D0680911

Turtles & Tortoises

By Russ Case

Karla Austin, *Business Operations Manager*
Nick Clemente, *Special Consultant*
Barbara Kimmel, *Managing Editor*
Jessica Knott, *Production Supervisor*
Cindy Weston, *Designer*
Melanie Irwin, *Design Concept*

Library of Congress Cataloging-in-Publication Data

Case, Russ.
  Turtles & tortoises / by Russ Case.
      p. cm. — (Beginning vivarium systems)
  ISBN-13: 978-1-882770-93-9
  ISBN-10: 1-882770-93-5

  1. Turtles as pets. I. Title. II. Title: Turtles and tortoises.

  SF459.T8C37 2007
  639.3'92—dc22

                              2006029681

2005036585

AVS ADVANCED VIVARIUM SYSTEMS™
An Imprint of BowTie Press®
3 Burroughs
Irvine, California 92618

Printed and bound in Singapore
16 15 14 13 12 11 10 09 08 07   1 2 3 4 5 6 7 8 9 10

Contents

Red-eared slider

CHAPTER 1

Reptiles as Pets

Compared with other animals, reptiles (including turtles, tortoises, lizards, and snakes) sometimes get a bum rap. Lots of people think reptiles—especially snakes—are slimy creatures that want to bite and squeeze them and maybe even use their fangs to inject them with poison. So when the time comes to choose a pet, millions of people pick animals that are friendlier.

Red-eared slider

Take dogs, for example. Dog owners can play and exercise with their pooches, brush their fur, dress them up, and perhaps even enter them in dog shows. There are special dog beaches and parks, where dog owners gather by the dozens. There you see dogs running all around, playing, barking, and having a great time—it's just like a kid's playground but hairier and with more slobber.

Dogs are loved because they give love back. They may lick people's faces, jump on them, sleep in their beds, and ride in their cars, and they want to be with their people all the time.

With reptiles, things are different. I've never been to a snake beach or a lizard park, where people frolic and play with their scaly pets. Turtles don't jump up and down when their owners come home from work. Lizards and turtles don't lick your face to show how much they love you, and I've never seen a tortoise riding in a car with its head hanging out the window and tongue flapping in the breeze. Pet reptiles

These Russian tortoises make good pets for beginners, including younger herpers.

aren't as interactive as dogs and some other pets are. A pet reptile may not want to be handled all the time, generally won't snuggle with you, and may not respond to your affection (although many tolerate some handling). Although reptiles are not usually interactive, they still can make great pets—especially for kids! On the following page are some reasons why.

Russian tortoise

Ten Reasons Reptiles Make Great Pets

If the adults in your house are not sure about adding a reptile to the family, ask them to consider the following points:

1. There are some great harmless beginner reptiles for kids to keep.

2. Compared with other pets, reptiles are low maintenance.

3. The risk of injury to responsible children is much lower than the risk of a dog bite, a cat scratch, or even a peck from a parakeet or nip from a hamster.

4. Reptiles are quiet.

5. The foods reptiles eat are readily available at pet shops and grocery stores.

6. Reptiles don't have to be fed every single day (but they shouldn't be starved).

7. Reptiles aren't hairy and don't have dander, so they make great pets for people with allergies.

8. Reptiles are easier to care for than almost any other pet.

9. Keeping reptiles teaches young owners responsibility and can help them grow into sensitive, caring adults.

10. Reptiles are really cool—just ask your kids!

Black-knobbed map turtle

Superpopular Pets

Reptiles have become super-popular over the past several years. Go to any pet store, and you'll see what I mean. For one thing, you'll find many different species, or types, of herps.

At pet stores, in addition to seeing lots of cool reptiles, you'll find oodles of stuff to help you take care of pet herps.

Lots of companies sell products that make it easy to provide pet reptiles with happy homes. They include different types of lights, gizmos to keep your herps warm, branches for them to climb on, cages to keep them in, and bowls for their water and food. (In chapters 4 and 5, you can read more about items such as these.)

There are even pet stores that sell only reptiles. You won't find dogs, parakeets, tropical fish, or cats there, but you are likely to see many different species of turtles and tortoises, lizards, frogs, snakes, and other really interesting animals.

People have been keeping pet herps for decades, but since 1993 the hobby has become

What's a Herp?

Herp is a nickname for a reptile or an amphibian, and it comes from the word *herpetology,* which means the study of reptiles and amphibians. A scientist who studies these animals is called a herpetologist.

really popular. I can tell you why: it is because of the movie *Jurassic Park.* I don't just write books about reptiles. I am also the editor of *Reptiles* magazine, and the fact that the magazine came out at about the same time as *Jurassic Park* was really lucky! People saw the movie, loved it, and as a result many wanted to learn about reptiles and how to keep them.

Reptile keeping has become very popular over the years.

Young people's interest in dinosaurs often leads to an interest in keeping pet reptiles.

Dinosaurs are fascinating. Of course, it's impossible to keep one as a pet. (If you could find one, it would probably be really expensive, and it scares me to think how expensive it would be to feed it.) Many people think the next best thing to having their own little T. rex is to own a pet lizard. And although it's great that so many people became interested in reptiles after seeing *Jurassic Park*, there was a sad side to their new popularity.

A pet turtle might be the next best thing to a pet dinosaur!

Galapagos tortoise

Something You Should Never Do

After Jurassic Park came out, many pet herps, including turtles and tortoises (but especially lizards), were bought on impulse by people who didn't know how to take proper care of them. The movie *Teenage Mutant Ninja Turtles* also caused a big demand for pet chelonians. People would (and still do) see a neat-looking reptile in a store and buy it right then and there. After all, these animals are very interesting, and some are really colorful. Impulse buyers take their new pets home and just put them in cages, where they often slowly fade away. Even today, many reptiles die or end up in animal shelters because of this. That is why you should never buy a pet reptile on impulse.

If you're a smart, caring owner, you'll have a lot of fun with your reptile pets—even though they won't fetch your slippers or the newspaper! So, congratulations if you've decided you want to take a shot at keeping them. Now, let's take a closer look at the world of turtles and tortoises, the reptiles you came here to read about!

Long, Long Time

Throughout this book, it is repeatedly pointed out that you should know how to house and care for a turtle or a tortoise before bringing one home. Something else to keep in mind is that these are long-lived animals. So you not only will need to know how to take care of a turtle or tortoise but also could end up having to do so for a long, long time. Aquatic turtles—turtles that spend most of their time in the water—can live for more than 40 years. Some tortoises can live to be 100! So keep in mind that if you get a pet turtle or tortoise, it could be with you for a very long time.

The *Teenage Mutant Ninja Turtles* inspired many people to buy turtles on impulse, which was unfortunate.

CHAPTER 2

What Chelonians Look Like

Turtles and tortoises are also called **chelonians** (keh-LO-nee-enz). Chelonians are reptiles, as are snakes and lizards. Although people don't all agree on how long turtles and tortoises have been on Earth, one estimate has them here for the past 200 million years. There are currently about 300 chelonian **species** alive today.

Western painted turtles

What is the difference between a turtle and a tortoise? Generally speaking, turtles spend most of their time in the water, and tortoises live on land. An animal that lives on land is *terrestrial*; one that lives in the water is *aquatic*. Thus, many turtles are called **aquatic**, or water, turtles. This doesn't mean they never come out of the water—all of them do at one time or another. Even the sea turtles, which live in the ocean, come out of the water to lay their eggs.

Ornate box turtle

Turtles are considered aquatic because they live in the water.

There are exceptions to the rule, however. Box turtles, for instance, differ from other turtles in that they live on land primarily and do not enter water as regularly as their aquatic cousins do. Also going against the norm

are the tortoises, such as hingeback tortoises, that live in moist areas.

Although they may prefer different types of **habitats**, turtles and tortoises are both immediately recognizable by one feature no other reptile has—a shell. Shells can vary quite a bit from species to species. Other body parts, such as feet, can as well. So let's take a look at the various physical features of chelonians.

What's a Habitat?

A habitat is the type of place an animal naturally lives, such as the ocean, the grassland, or the desert.

Turtle Stories

The word *chelonian* comes from the Greek. According to Greek mythology, Chelone was a nymph (a minor goddess) who turned down an invitation to attend the wedding of Zeus and Hera (think of them as the royalty of all the Greek gods). She preferred not to leave her house to come to the wedding, and this was considered a great insult. To teach Chelone a lesson, Zeus turned her into a tortoise. By doing that, he forced her to always carry her house on her back—which, as you probably know, tortoises and turtles do to this day.

Tortoises and turtles play important roles in many cultures around the world. According to some Native American legends, the world was built on the back of a giant turtle. A Chinese legend links Nu Kua, the goddess who created people, with chelonians. It says she took four toes from a titanic tortoise (sometimes called the cosmic tortoise) and used them to form the four compass points of north, south, east, and west.

Then there's the fable by Aesop called *The Tortoise and the Hare*, in which the tortoise wins a race against the much faster hare by being slow and deliberate, rather than fast and careless. This fable led not only to the well-known saying "Slow and steady wins the race" but also to some cartoon versions of the story, including one by Walt Disney and another starring Bugs Bunny. Thanks in large part to Aesop's fable, tortoises in other stories have often been portrayed as wise old creatures.

You can see that turtles and tortoises have been an important part of many people's beliefs, and they have been used to teach some important lessons.

Wondrous Shells

A shell provides turtles and tortoises with shelter and protection. You may think the shell is only the top part of a turtle's body, but it actually wraps around the entire body, top and bottom. The top part of the shell is called the **carapace**. The bottom part, or the underside of the animal, is called the **plastron**.

Both the carapace and the plastron are made of many bones that are fused together and

Softshell turtles have leathery shells, not hard shells like other species'.

attached to the turtle's spine and rib cage. The shell is covered with **scutes**, which are plates that form a protective layer that works like a shield. It is the scutes you are looking at when you look at a turtle or tortoise.

All chelonians have shells, but not all their shells are the same. For instance, there are softshell turtles. The carapace of these flat turtles is missing the hard scutes and is instead leathery and flexible.

This is the plastron of a Western painted turtle. It looks painted, doesn't it?

What Are Scutes?

Scutes, which cover the shells of chelonians, are made of keratin, the same substance that makes our fingernails. Think of scutes as big and protective fingernails.

Box turtle shells are hinged so they can close up tight.

There's a really big turtle that doesn't have a hard carapace. The leatherback sea turtle can grow to 8 feet (2.5 meters) in length and weigh about 1,500 pounds (6,805 kilograms). This huge turtle is called leatherback because its back is covered with leathery skin (and bones to support it).

Box turtles have unique shells, too. They are called box turtles because they can completely close themselves up inside their shells. The plastron of a box turtle is hinged on the bottom, which allows it to close up tightly against the carapace after the turtle has pulled in its head, legs, and tail. People have had their fingers caught inside box turtle shells. To get a turtle to open up its shell, it has to be placed in a bucket of water. The sudden immersion in water can surprise the turtle into opening up—not to mention that it needs to breathe air and will open up to do so. Needless to say, I don't recommend that you go poking your fingers into any box turtles' shells. It's not nice to do that anyway.

Looking at Shells

Turtles and tortoises are instantly recognizable by their shells. But not all carapaces are alike. Here are some colorful examples of the variety of shells out there:

The red-footed tortoise's shell is dark with reddish yellow spots.

The leopard tortoise gets its name from the leopardlike pattern of its shell.

This is a yellow-blotched map turtle from southern Mississippi.

The diamondback terrapin has a very distinctive shell pattern.

Red-eared sliders come in different colors. This is a pastel slider.

This red-eared slider's shell and body are deformed.

Turtles and tortoises can't leave their shells the way, for instance, a hermit crab can. A hermit crab is not attached to its shell, so as it grows larger, it must leave its shell and find a larger one. A chelonian shell, however, is actually attached to the animal—the shell grows as the animal grows. Some unlucky chelonians though, have shells that don't grow. These deformed shells can look like twisted little caps on top of the poor turtle's back. Pet animals may survive, at least for a while, with such deformities, but any time a wild animal's typical appearance and form of protection is changed, its life is put at risk because predators may zero in on it. A healthy shell, however, grows right along with its owner.

The shape of the carapace can vary. Aquatic turtles are usually somewhat flattened, which makes it easier for them to swim through the water. Most tortoise shells and box turtle shells, however, are usually higher and shaped more like a dome or a bell. There is one tortoise with a flat carapace, and it's actually called the pancake tortoise. (See chapter 8.)

Something else about the shell: it often leads to pet chelonians being named Shelley and Sheldon.

Feet and Flippers

Another physical characteristic that some turtles have that no other reptile has is flippers. Most chelonians have feet—tortoises have strong legs with big toenails.

Box turtles have fairly stumpy feet. And some male aquatic turtles have feet with long claws. But sea turtles have flippers.

Sea turtles are wondrous animals. (Read more about them in chapter 10.) They have

Birds Aren't the Only Ones with Beaks

You probably know that birds have beaks, but did you know other animals do, too? Yep, turtles and tortoises have beaks (so do octopuses and squid!). Unlike their reptilian cousins the snakes and lizards, turtles and tortoises don't have teeth. Instead, they have beaks that they use to bite food. The beak is a horny, jagged structure, which some turtles and tortoises can use to give you a good bite if you're not careful. A friend and I once watched one of my desert tortoises very slowly walk up to my friend's bare foot and stretch out its neck, also very slowly, to take a nip at my friend's toe!

Some turtles are famous for their ability to bite. Snapping turtles aren't called snappers for nothing! There are two kinds of snappers: the common snapping turtle and the alligator snapping turtle. Take a guess as to which one is bigger and more powerful. The name *alligator* should have given it away.

strong flippers that allow them to swim through the ocean. They're not the only turtles with flippers, though. One other turtle has flippers—the pig-nosed turtle, also known as the Fly River turtle. This is one interesting turtle. It is a freshwater turtle that lives in Australia and New Guinea. It is interesting not only because it has flippers (each flipper has two claws, unlike a sea turtle's) but also because of its longish piggy nose.

Aquatic turtles have webbed feet that enable them to swim.

Sea turtle

As mentioned, some males have long claws. This is one way you can tell male emydid turtles (such as red-ears and painteds) from females. The males use their claws during courtship, when they stretch out their front legs and "fan" their claws by vibrating them rapidly on the sides of a female turtle's face. The long claws are also used to grasp the female's shell during actual mating.

Tortoise feet are equipped with powerful toenails. These allow tortoises, which live on land rather than in water, to dig burrows and nests. They find shelter in burrows, to avoid heat, and dig nests before laying eggs. Imagine doing all that if you didn't have strong toenails!

I use my claws to rip my food apart.

Red-eared slider

Feet and Flippers Up Close

Chelonian feet come in different shapes and sizes—even different forms. Sea turtles have flippers! Check out these examples:

Western painted turtles have webbed feet to help them swim. Like red-eared sliders, they are aquatic turtles.

The feet of softshell turtles appear more flipperlike than the feet of other aquatic turtles, such as painteds and red-ears.

This green sea turtle's powerful flippers help the turtle navigate its ocean habitat as well as dig nests on beaches.

Box turtles have stumpy legs and feet that are more tortoiselike than turtlelike.

Long Necks

Chelonians have fairly long necks, but some have longer necks than others. Aquatic turtles have long necks that help them breathe when they're under water. A turtle may be sitting on the bottom of a shallow pond or in an aquarium in your home, and it will stretch its neck out until its nostrils peek just out of the water so the turtle can breathe. It may remain like this for some time, breathing air while most of its body is submerged.

There is a group of turtles well known for the length of their necks. These are the snake-necked and side-necked turtles from Australia, New Guinea, and South America. As their names indicate, these turtles have really long necks. Some have necks that are longer than their shells! This is a hassle for the turtles when they need to pull their heads into their shells for protection—they can't.

Can you guess why this species is called a snake-necked turtle?

Other Physical Features

Chelonian heads and legs are covered with scales and skin. Some tortoise skin (such as that of the Galapagos tortoise) is quite tough and can resemble elephant skin. The tough skin of some desert species, such as the desert tortoises of the United States and the spurred tortoise of Africa (also known as the sulcata tortoise), helps them retain precious moisture in their super-hot habitats. Like other reptiles, chelonians shed their skin. If you keep aquatic turtles, you may see pieces of skin coming off their legs and necks. This is normal, so don't be worried if you see it happening to your turtles. Tortoises usually shed their skin in patches.

Turtles use their long necks to catch food and breathe air.

Instead of pulling their heads into their shells, these turtles have to fold their heads along the side of their shells, between the carapace and the plastron. That's why some are called side-necked turtles.

Some tortoises have long necks, too, which they stretch out to grab leaves off bushes. Galapagos tortoises, real giants in the chelonian world (read more about them in chapter 8), can stretch their necks way out to bite a tasty leaf off a tall bush.

What Is Ectothermic?

Turtles and tortoises are **ectothermic**, which means they depend on the environment to raise and lower their body temperature.

Side-necked turtles tuck their heads alongside their bodies for protection.

Unlike snakes, but like most lizards, chelonians have eyelids that they close when sleeping and to protect their eyes. Like all other herps, turtles don't have ears that stick out. But although lizards have an external membrane leading to the inner ear, turtles do not. It looks as if chelonians have no ears at all, but they do have an inner ear, and they respond to vibrations and low-frequency sounds.

Now you know some stories regarding the history of turtles and tortoises and a thing or two about their bodies. In the next chapter, we'll take a look at the places you can observe turtles and tortoises as well as purchase chelonians. You will also get some hints about how to treat nature and to tell if a pet store has healthy animals.

Desert tortoise

A Turtle's Other Name

All living things are known by both common names and scientific names. Scientific names are usually in Latin, although sometimes they originate from the Greek. The two words that make up an animal's Latin name are the genus (first word) and the species (second word). There can be more than one species within a genus. For instance, the wood turtle's scientific name is *Clemmys* (genus) *insculpta* (species), and the spotted turtle's is *Clemmys guttata*. Note that they are two different species within the same genus.

The species name often reveals something about the animal. In the case of the wood turtle mentioned above, *insculpta* means "carved," and it is so named because its shell looks as if it's been carved from wood.

A subspecies occurs when an animal is different from others of its species but not enough to reclassify it as a new species. Where the animal lives can play a part. For instance, the painted turtle is *Chrysemys picta*. The eastern painted turtle is *Chrysemys (genus) picta* (species) *picta* (subspecies), and the western painted turtle is *Chrysemys picta belli*.

Did you know that we are *Homo sapiens*? Roughly translated, that means "human being." *Homo* is Latin for "human," and *sapiens* is Latin for "intelligent." So *Homo sapiens* means "intelligent human."

Your common name most likely means something, too. For instance, my name is Russ, which is short for Russell, which means "redhead." Can you guess what color my hair used to be before it began turning gray?

CHAPTER 3

Where to Find Turtles & Tortoises

P eople find pet chelonians in different places. Pet stores immediately come to mind, of course. They are where many turtles and tortoises can be purchased, and we will get to pet stores in a bit. You can also buy turtles and tortoises from breeders and at reptile expos or get them at shelters. Then there's the possibility of buying them online. First, though, let's go to the source—the place where these animals actually live.

Red-eared slider

Nature

Imagine this: You're hiking along the side of a beautiful stream. You're enjoying the sunshine and having a wonderful time exploring the great outdoors with your friends. A breeze is blowing, the stream is gurgling, and the air smells fresh and clean. You turn a corner and there, basking on a log overhanging the stream, is a turtle, maybe a red-eared slider or a painted turtle. You stop, hush your friends, and approach the turtle as quietly as you can, tiptoeing up to it while trying to make yourself as invisible as possible. The turtle remains on its log, soaking up some welcome sunshine, and you continue your sneaky approach. Your friends are watching closely. You are within grabbing distance, and you begin to reach out toward the turtle. The turtle instantly dives into the water. You see it paddle furiously to the bottom of the river, where it disappears from view. Then it pops its head out of the water a distance away, as if to say, "Ha! Missed me!"

Don't Take Box Turtles

I mentioned box turtles and their unique shells in chapter 2. These turtles are found in states all along the east coast of the United States and as far west as Texas. They are popular pets, and they are truly great turtles. However, wild box turtle populations are suffering big-time, and I don't recommend that any be taken from the wild.

If you find a wild box turtle while you're hiking outdoors, please resist the temptation to

take it home. Look at it, photograph it, but please leave any wild box turtle where you find it. You can buy captive-bred box turtles, and they're likely healthier and easier to care for anyway.

Many aquatic turtles, such as these red-ears, spend a lot of time basking in the sun. They will drop into the water at the first sign of danger.

To anyone who has searched for turtles in nature (also known as the wild), this may be a familiar scene. Of course, the turtle doesn't always get away. Often the result is the successful capture of a wild chelonian. Many reptile owners started off catching their own pets, long before they began buying them in stores. As a kid, I spent hours searching for herps in the woods near my New Jersey home and later in Southern California. No matter where you live in the United States, there may be some reptiles and amphibians living near you. They may not be right in your backyard, especially if you live in a big city with more cement and buildings than fields and woods. But they may still be found within driving distance.

Map turtle

Photo Op

Some people take photos of reptiles instead of catching them to bring home as pets. Reptile photography is a fun hobby, and this may be something you would enjoy as a "sideline" to your interest in reptiles.

Where and When to Go

Looking for reptiles in the wild is called herping, and there are several ways to go about it. The first is to go hiking in a place where you're likely to find some reptiles. Woods, desert areas,

Desert blooms may attract desert tortoises.

Always Respect Nature

Not everyone who looks along the edges of streams, ponds, and swamps for turtles is out to catch them and bring them home to keep as pets. Many people like finding turtles and tortoises in the wild simply to watch them.

Whenever you are out in nature, try to disturb the wildlife as little as possible. Don't trample on and break plants as you hike. And if you turn over any rocks or logs, put them back the way you found them. Never litter, and always plan to bring home anything you took with you into wild areas.

"Leave nothing but footprints" is a favorite saying among nature lovers. This means there should be no sign that you were ever in the wild—no candy wrappers, empty water bottles, broken branches, or disturbed areas. Always try to leave things the way you found them. Remember that just because you may not see them doesn't mean animals don't live in these areas. And these animals don't want their homes (even if it's just a rock) to be destroyed or pushed over as you pass through their "neighborhoods."

Red-footed tortoises live in humid climates in South America.

parks—nearly anywhere that hasn't been bulldozed to make room for buildings. If you're looking for turtles, you should focus on woodsy areas with lakes, ponds, and other watery places. If you're looking for tortoises, go to dry, scrubby areas, including actual deserts.

Certain times of the year are better for herping than others are. You won't usually find herps if you look for them during the winter, for instance, especially if you live in an area that gets really cold outside. This is because they'll be hibernating, safely tucked away, while you waste your time stomping about looking for them. If you do manage to find some while they're hibernating—well, it's just rude, and possibly unhealthy for the animals, to disturb them.

Spring, summer, and early fall are usually the best times to have successful herping adventures.

Don't take box turtles out of the woods!

What to Take with You

Before you start hiking, get your outdoor herping adventures off to a good start by buying a good field guide. There are several reptile and amphibian field guides readily available in bookstores. (See the Recommended Reading section at the end of this book.)

Field guides include photos and drawings of animals you're likely to find in different areas within the United States or other countries. You'll also find **range** information, often including maps, that tells where the

Desert tortoises may be found in U.S. deserts, but don't remove them.

different species of turtles and tortoises can be found. Range information gives you an idea of what you may expect to find in any area in any state. This type of information is especially useful because some turtles look similar to each other. If you find one and look it up in your field guide, the range information may help you identify it.

Youngsters should never venture off into the woods alone under any circumstances. Adults should join in, and a fun family outing can be enjoyed by all. Adults will also be able to help you make the right choices about what to wear and take on a hike. And don't forget a camera!

No Trespassing

Always be careful about trespassing while herping. If necessary, get a property owner's permission to look for chelonians on his or her land. If you just climb a fence or enter a gate without asking, you could find yourself in trouble, especially if the angry property owner couldn't care less about turtles or tortoises!

Herping Gear

If you go herping in the wild, a good field guide is one item you will want to go with you, but there is other stuff you may want to take along as well. If you're hiking outside during the day, you may need insect repellent, sunscreen, water, and other standard gear you would take on a hike. Check with someone who is experienced in hiking, such as a knowledgeable clerk at a sporting goods store, to decide what you should take with you. What you take often depends on the type of area you're going to and the length of the hike.

Hats and protective clothing, such as long-sleeved shirts and pants, may be needed. Remember that you may be hiking through wild areas that contain plants with scratchy branches. Wearing short-sleeved shirts and shorts could result in cuts and scratches, or sunburn if you forget your sunscreen. While looking for aquatic turtles, you might be walking in water—rubber boots will keep your feet dry.

Here's a suggestion for what to take for a day of herping:

- ☑ **Camera**
- ☑ **Field guide**
- ☑ **Hiking gear**
- ☑ **Protective clothing**
- ☑ **Old shoes you don't mind getting wet (for wading)**
- ☑ **Sunscreen**
- ☑ **Water**

Don't Break Any Laws

Depending on where you live, it may be against the law to catch wild reptiles and bring them home, especially if they are **endangered species**. (See chapter 10 for information on endangered turtles and tortoises.) You may need a permit, a fishing license, or both to legally collect some wild reptiles. So before you go out to catch any reptiles, check your local laws. (You may need to have an adult help you with this.)

Go about your herp hunting the legal way. A good place to start your research is at your city's government Web sites. You can also check with your local Fish and Game office (Fish and Game is a government organization that enforces laws about fish and animals). Dig around a little and you'll soon know what you

Alligators frequent the same habitat that some aquatic turtles do.

can and cannot catch legally.

National parks, which are owned and operated by the government, are beautiful places to observe nature. Some of the most famous U.S. national parks include Yellowstone National Park, in Wyoming; Yosemite National Park, in California; and Everglades National Park, in Florida. You can find reptiles—and often lots of other animals—in all of these parks. Keep in mind, however, that you are not permitted to capture and take any animal, turtles and tortoises included, from a national park. These parks are definitely where you should just observe the animals in their natural habitats and take pictures of them.

Never remove any animal from a national park such as Yosemite.

Pet Stores

Pet stores are where you go when you want to see exotic reptiles that you can't find while hiking around areas near your house. A store may be the first place you'll see many different species of chelonians. Some pet stores, including the big pet superstores, sell lots of animals, and reptiles may be just one type that you see in such stores. Not far from the reptile section, you may be able to look at dogs, kittens, hamsters, or tropical fish.

It's fun to look at reptiles in pet stores. I remember seeing my first turtles in stores years ago. Back in those days, stores could sell all species of baby turtles, and many different varieties were

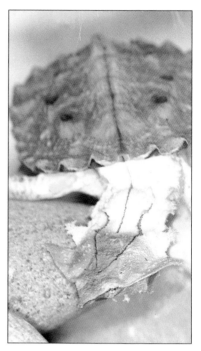

The South American mata mata's unique shape helps camouflage it.

available. I used to see them a lot not only in regular pet stores but also in tropical fish stores. Some that I kept back then were sidenecked turtles, map turtles, redeared sliders, musk turtles, and painted turtles. My brother even got a baby mata mata. I named it Gamera after a Japanese movie monster—a giant turtle that could fly through the air. (Learn more about the mata mata in chapter 7.) These days, there are more rules about selling baby turtles, mostly because of a disease

What Is an Endangered Species?

A species is considered to be endangered when there are so few members alive that the species is in danger of dying out. You should never capture an endangered species.

Stores that sell reptiles usually sell a variety of useful reptile supplies as well.

called salmonellosis, caused by a bacterium called *Salmonella* (see the box on page 109).

Pet stores, of course, also sell many of the supplies you will need to keep your pet turtles and tortoises healthy (supplies are covered in chapters 4 and 5). You can often buy live food, too, such as worms, from pet stores. So stores are good places to go shopping not just for your actual pet but also for everything your pet will need to live a healthy life.

Then there are the reptile-only stores. The number and variety of reptiles at these stores are usually larger than those of stores selling other kinds of animals, so there are more to choose from. The owners of reptile-only stores sometimes breed reptiles, too.

Both types of store can be excellent places to purchase pet tortoises and turtles. No

Beware of stores that crowd their turtles into unhealthy conditions like this!

Nasal and eye discharge are sure signs of illness in turtles and tortoises.

matter which type you choose to visit, however, you should look for cleanliness, healthy animals, and a knowledgeable staff. Use these three tips when deciding whether to buy a tortoise or a turtle from a store:

Clean Places

A clean store with clean cages often means the animals are healthy. Cleanliness results in better animal health, whether you're talking about reptiles or giraffes. If you visit a store and the cages contain rotting, uneaten food or old animal poop—and if the cages stink— then think twice about buying any turtles or tortoises from that store because there's a greater chance that they may be sick.

Don't Buy Sick Ones

Some people buy sick reptiles thinking they can help the animals get well. Don't do it! If the turtle or tortoise even lives long enough, you'll probably just end up spending a lot of money on veterinary bills and medicine. There's no guarantee a sick reptile will get well under your care. Why start off with such a problem? Buy only healthy animals.

Captive-Bred Versus Wild-Caught Animals

Whether a turtle or a tortoise was bred in captivity or caught in the wild is helpful to know when you're shopping for one.

Captive-bred chelonians are a great choice for a few reasons. First, they are often healthier and less likely to be infected with disease or parasites (little buglike creatures that can live on or in your pets). They are often more used to captivity than wild chelonians, which are captured and eventually shipped to the pet store. Turtles and tortoises that go through this process can be stressed out, which can lead to sickness.

Red-footed tortoise

There are many species of chelonians being bred in captivity, including some that make the best pets, such as red-footed tortoises and red-eared sliders. You may find that captive-bred animals are more expensive than wild-caught ones, but many reptile keepers think the additional price is worth it.

Also, by buying captive-bred chelonians, especially tortoises and box turtles, you are helping to protect the environment. It's bad for nature if too many animals are removed from their habitats to be shipped away and sold as pets. For every captive-bred tortoise that is sold, though, that's one less tortoise that was taken out of nature. That's a great thing!

Not all species of turtles and tortoises are captive-bred regularly, so if you want a particular species, you might have to get one that's caught in the wild. Wild-caught reptiles can make fine pets. They may need more time to settle down in captivity, and they may have some health issues that captive-bred animals don't (a veterinarian can help with this). This doesn't mean a captive-bred animal comes with a 100-percent health guarantee, either, but its chances are better.

Healthy Turtles and Tortoises

Chapter 9 covers health, but you need to know how to spot an unhealthy chelonian in a store. Let's discuss briefly the signs of sick turtles and tortoises.

Healthy chelonians are active and alert, with bright eyes. If you see one with eyes that are sunken or watery and skin that looks kind of shriveled up, then it's not healthy. Look at its nostrils as well. Are there bubbles around them or maybe some liquid discharge

Before you buy a pet, make sure it is healthy and has a hearty appetite.

Return Guarantees

Many pet stores and some reptile breeders will guarantee their animals during a certain time frame. They will give you another animal or a credit if something happens to the one you bought. Ask before you buy.

from the nostrils or eyes? Never buy such an animal because it may have a respiratory infection, which would make it hard for the animal to breathe properly.

Sometimes a turtle or tortoise may look healthy but not actually be healthy. One way to tell if the animal is healthy or not is to find out whether it's eating. Ask a store employee to feed it while you watch. If it has just eaten, come back later when it's ready to eat again. If the turtle or tortoise eats readily, that's a good sign.

As mentioned, a healthy chelonian is alert. If you see one that is looking around, seems interested in its surroundings, and aware of things, then that's a good sign. A

To avoid potential problems, inspect turtles top and bottom before purchasing.

sleeping animal may not necessarily be ill, but alertness and bright eyes are signs of health.

If you find a turtle or tortoise you want to buy, ask to see it close-up. Give it a quick inspection for any injuries or abnormalities on the shell, both top and bottom. Look for stuff coming out of its nose, eyes, or vent (its butt, in other words). There shouldn't be anything stuck to these areas or oozing out of them. The skin should be clear of anything that doesn't look normal. Look in the areas where the legs go into the shell, and make sure there's nothing abnormal there.

An alert turtle or tortoise that doesn't have any skin or shell abnormalities, is clean, and is eating is a good choice to buy. However, it's always a good idea to take any new pet reptile to a veterinarian for a checkup just to be sure there isn't something wrong inside the animal.

Knowledgeable Staff

Some pet store employees work there because they like animals and know a lot about them. Others just need a job. Whenever possible, it's best to find a store with people who know about the animals. Store staff should also be willing to help you and answer questions even after you get your turtle or tortoise home. Ask ahead of time what a store's policy is regarding this and what kind of guarantee it offers on its animals (in case your new pet gets sick or dies).

A pet store with knowledgeable and helpful staff can play a big part in your reptile-keeping experiences. Such a store can make all the difference, too, in whether you want to continue keeping turtles or not. That's a big responsibility, and the better stores take it seriously. Other stores may be interested only in getting your money, so choose your stores wisely!

Reptile Breeders and Reptile Expos

When you're looking at reptiles in pet stores, do you ever wonder where they came from? There are three likely places: (1) they were caught in the wild, maybe in a far-off country, and shipped to the pet store; (2) the owner of the store bred them personally; or (3) they were sold to the pet store by a professional reptile breeder.

Many people breed reptiles, and some of them make a lot of money doing so. I think this would be a fun job. Some breed only turtles or tortoises, some breed only lizards, and others

Some shops sell reptiles and nothing else!

prefer to breed snakes. Others breed lots of different reptiles and maybe even some frogs.

You can often buy tortoises and turtles directly from the people who breed them. Many professional reptile breeders have Web sites, where you can learn all about the breeders and their animals and get other information. Some provide care tips for the animals they breed and

Buying Chelonians on the Internet

You can often buy pet turtles and tortoises directly from reptile breeders who have Web sites. You can also buy directly from reptile dealers who may import wild-caught animals that aren't being bred in captivity.

Buying a reptile over the Internet is different from buying one in a pet store. The biggest difference, obviously, is that you can walk into a pet store and inspect the turtle or tortoise you want to buy in person. If you find a turtle or tortoise you want to buy on a Web site, you have to rely on pictures of it and the word of the dealer to determine whether you really want to get it.

Dealers should be patient and willing to offer good care advice and guarantees on their reptiles. You can sometimes ask around, including posting questions on the Internet, about whether an Internet reptile dealer is a good one or not. You may need to have someone familiar with Internet chat rooms and message boards help you, but if you find a dealer online who has a turtle or tortoise that you want, it's a good idea to try to find out if that dealer has a good reputation or a bad one.

You can also ask online dealers to provide references with whom you can speak; these are people with whom they have previously done business and who had no problems as a result.

Expos are great places to buy herps and meet herp people, including breeders.

sell; some sell supplies, T-shirts, and other reptile stuff.

Many reptile breeders sell animals at reptile shows, or expos. If you've never been to a reptile expo, you really should go. You can find listings for upcoming shows in *Reptiles* magazine, as well as on the Internet, in newspapers, and other places.

A reptile expo is usually held in a big hall with a bunch of booths and tables where reptile breeders sell their reptiles. There are big expos and small ones, and the big ones can attract hundreds of breeders selling lots of different types of reptiles. Expos pop up all over the world. Currently, the biggest one in the United States, the National Reptile Breeders' Expo, takes place in Daytona Beach, Florida, every August. Many cities, however, host reptile expos. Some are put together by reptile clubs; others are organized by professional companies. There are European reptile expos, too (Germany has some big ones).

You can learn a lot at a reptile expo. You are surrounded by people who like reptiles, and you can talk to breeders. Sometimes you can sit in on lectures that are given by well-known reptile experts. Contests and other fun activities may be held, and some expos have all types of reptiles for sale. And there are lots of turtles and tortoises, of course! You'll see them in big plastic tubs or aquariums, swimming and walking around, often with a bunch of chelonian enthusiasts watching them.

Now that you know where to get your pet chelonians, it's time to learn about the type of equipment you will need to maintain them properly. And it just so happens that is what the next chapter is all about. Read on!

Shelters and Rescues

Some turtles and tortoises escape from their homes, and others are "set free" on purpose by irresponsible owners who no longer want them. Either situation can be very sad.

Some lost animals end up in animal shelters or with rescue organizations, places that will care for them and try to find them homes. Sometimes pet owners who can no longer care for their pets, or who no longer want to, will bring their animals to these places, hoping the people working at the shelter will find new homes for their pets.

Occasionally, turtles and tortoises end up at shelters. They may have grown too large for their owners to properly care for them, or they were "rescued" from the wild by well-meaning people. Other times, injured turtles, perhaps one that was dinged by a passing car or nicked by a lawn mower, are taken to rescues.

If you can provide a homeless pet with a new home, that's a great thing. For that reason, keep these places in mind if you want a pet turtle or tortoise. There are even special desert tortoise rescues, which we will cover in more detail in chapter 8. Remember, though, that bringing home a sick animal is usually not a good idea, especially if you're a young, inexperienced reptile keeper.

CHAPTER 4

Making a Good Turtle Home

Years ago, the enclosure of choice for a baby aquatic turtle (which was usually a red-eared slider) was a small plastic tabletop pool. In the middle of the pool was an island with a little plastic palm tree, a tiny cuplike area for some gravel, and a built-in ramp leading out of the water.

Musk turtle

Unfortunately, many baby turtles met their doom while being kept in these inadequate enclosures. Back then, people didn't know about feeding the right foods, using the proper lighting, and providing the right type of turtle-friendly habitat. Luckily, turtle enthusiasts have learned a lot since then, and turtles today have a much better chance of surviving in captivity as long as their owners take the time to keep them properly.

In this chapter, you'll learn the basic points of proper turtle housing. (The following chapter will tell you how to make a proper home for tortoises.) All the equipment mentioned in this chapter, including aquariums, aquarium filters, siphons, and silicone sealant, can be purchased at stores that sell reptile and tropical fish supplies.

Roomy Places to Live

Many beginners who want to keep turtles and tortoises don't realize that these reptiles need a lot of room to do well in captivity. Some species can get

Red-eared sliders grow quite large and need a lot of space to swim.

pretty big, and if they're cramped into enclosures that are too small for them, they won't thrive. They'll get sick and possibly die. Even if you have a large enclosure, avoid overcrowding. It's much better to have a couple of healthy turtles swimming happily in a roomy home than to have six turtles that can barely move. A 60-gallon (227-liter [L]) aquarium can comfortably house two full-grown aquatic turtles.

Knowing how big a turtle or tortoise will eventually become will help you decide whether you will be able to house it properly. I will provide the adult sizes of some chelonians that make good pets in chapters 7 and 8.

Red-eared slider

Watery Homes for Aquatic Turtles

Naturally, for aquatic turtles you need to provide an enclosure that holds water. If you can keep turtles outside, which gives them the health benefits of the sun, you can construct an outdoor turtle pool. (See the activity section in this chapter to learn how to build one.) Although outdoor pools can be great homes for aquatic turtles, indoor aquariums are the most popular homes for them. Whichever you choose, be sure to set up the turtle enclosure before you bring any turtles home.

The bottom of your aquarium can contain gravel, such as

Watch the water depth when setting up an aquatic enclosure.

the type used in tropical fish tanks; larger stones, such as river rock; or nothing at all. Having nothing in the bottom may not look as natural and pretty as gravel or rocks, but it does make it easier to clean the tank. If you do use gravel or rocks, clean and rinse them thoroughly before putting them in your turtle tank.

The depth of the water depends on the species of turtle you want to keep. Some, such as sliders, painted turtles, and map turtles, are excellent swimmers, so the water depth in their tanks can be fairly deep. Other species, such as mud and musk turtles, aren't strong swimmers, so their water should be shallower. Remember: even though they spend a lot of time underwater, turtles still need to breathe air. You want to make it easy for them to do so, even when they're swimming. A turtle shouldn't have to paddle furiously to stay afloat at the same time it's trying to breathe.

You can also provide floating objects that your turtles can rest on, such as plastic plants that are sold for use in tropical fish tanks. (Be sure they're built solidly, just in case your turtles become curious and chew on them.)

The water you fill the aquarium with needs to be conditioned before you introduce your pets to their new home. Although you and I may not be affected by certain chemicals found in tap water, they can affect animals such as turtles and fish that spend all their time in the water. Water conditioners make tap water safe for these creatures. Products made especially for turtles are available at pet stores, and these are recommended. After purchasing a water conditioner, use it for a couple of days before you bring your turtle home.

When they are not basking, red-eared sliders spend a lot of time in the water.

Aquarium filters can also be used to keep water clean. There are many different types, including undergravel filters and canister filters. Talk to store employees to find out which type of filter they recommend for your turtle tank. The type of filter you use makes a difference in how you set up your tank (whether you have

Depth

Here's a good rule of thumb when deciding how deep the water should be in your aquarium: the turtle should be able to stand on the bottom of the tank on its hind legs, extend its neck, and be able to breathe easily at the water's surface.

Snapping turtle

gravel on the bottom or nothing at all, for instance) and how deep the water needs to be.

Places for Landlubbers

Some turtle keepers set up their aquatic turtle tanks so that a land area is available to the turtles. This can be done by piling gravel behind some rocks or driftwood on one side of the tank. The rocks act like a dam, keeping the gravel from slipping down into the water area. If you want to get fancy, you can use silicone sealant to attach glass to the bottom of the tank so that it creates a wall that separates the land from the water areas (younger enthusiasts should seek help from adults or older siblings when working with silicone and glass). Then fill the land section with rock and gravel. If you

attach the wall correctly, it should prevent any water from leaking over into the land area. Take your measurements for this wall to a hardware store that will cut the glass for you. Keep in mind that the height of this wall dictates how deep the water can be.

Another way to create a land area for your turtles is to put a plastic container full of rocks and gravel into the aquarium. Placing larger rocks in the bottom of the container and gravel on top of them aids drainage, which helps keep the top surface dry. The size of the container depends on how much land area you want to provide. Place it on the bottom of the aquarium, and add water to the aquarium (not the container) until it reaches the top edge of the container. The water level, as well as the level of the gravel in the container, should be sufficient to allow the turtles to easily climb from the water onto the gravel land area. Be sure that there's not enough space around the container to allow the turtle to wedge itself between the wall of the container and the wall of the aquarium.

With any of these methods, turtles should be able to climb from the water onto the land area. You might need to add a ramp—either an actual turtle ramp sold at pet stores for this purpose or one made of bark or smooth rocks and branches—to make it easy for them to do so.

Clean Your Turtle Tank

It is super, super ultraimportant to keep your turtle tank clean! Aquatic turtles are messy. They eat a lot and go to the bathroom a lot. Naturally, they go in the water. You can use aquarium filters and replace the water once a week to keep the water clean (don't forget to treat the new water to remove chemicals, as mentioned previously). You can also spot-clean turtle poop or uneaten food you see on the bottom using a gravel vacuum or siphon.

If you have gravel in the bottom of your tank, clean it thoroughly whenever you replace the water. This can be done by adding water to the tank until the gravel is covered, swirling the gravel around (you'll see the water get dirty), and pouring off the dirty water; repeat this until the water remains clean. Or you can remove the gravel from the tank and wash it separately in a bucket using the same rinsing process.

If you don't keep your turtle tank clean, it will quickly turn into a smelly, mucky soup that is unhealthy for your turtle. Dirty water can contribute to a nasty condition known as shell rot (read about it in chapter 9).

Haul-Out and Basking Areas

Wild aquatic turtles spend most of their time in the water, but they do come out to dry off and bask in the sun. This provides them with warmth and with important vitamins that keep them healthy. The vitamins help them utilize calcium, which is important for healthy shells and bones. For this reason, if you don't have a land area in your turtle tank, you need to have a haul-out so your turtles can haul themselves out of the water. This area should be large enough to allow the turtles to completely leave the water, without any part of them (such as their hind feet) still submerged. (Turtles look kind of funny when they're basking because they often stretch their hind legs way out.) It should be easy for the turtles to crawl out, too—they shouldn't have to struggle and strain.

Haul-out areas can be floating platforms made especially for turtles; branches that are wedged between the aquarium walls; smooth rocks, driftwood, cork platforms; or a combination of these objects. Just be sure the haul-outs allow your turtles to completely leave the water when they feel the need.

Provide basking lights near haul-out areas so turtles can warm up and dry off.

Basking lights provide heat; UVB lights promote health.

Important Lighting Tips

Place a basking light above land areas and haul-outs to provide heat for your turtles. There are many different types of basking lightbulbs available at pet and reptile stores. The staff there can help you choose the right one. The area beneath the basking light should be 85 to 89 degrees Fahrenheit (F) (29 to 32 degrees Celsius [C]). Don't place the light so close to your turtles that they could touch the bulb. Remember that some turtles can stretch their necks out pretty far, so you need to take that into consideration.

Always remember that younger enthusiasts should have adult guidance when working with lights and electricity.

If you keep your turtles indoors, you need full-spectrum ultraviolet fluorescent light tubes over the entire turtle tank. These provide health-giving rays that outdoor turtles get

What's UVB?

UVB stands for "ultraviolet B light." The sun emits this type of light (and others), which is essential for a turtle's health. You need to set up special lights for your indoor turtles so they can get UVB.

Lights for Health

For optimum turtle health, you should have two types of lights on your turtle tank: full-spectrum fluorescent lights over the entire length of the tank, and a heat-giving basking bulb placed over the basking area.

from the sun. Again, there are many different types. Make sure the tubes emit UVB, and ask pet store employees for help. Although fluorescent tubes may still light up, their health-giving properties wear out after several months. Check the packaging on the tubes to find out how often they should be replaced. (Read more about UVB in chapter 9, in the "Metabolic Bone Disease" section.)

Some aquariums come with glass covers. You don't need these for your turtle tank. If you place full-spectrum lights on top of a glass cover, the health-giving UVB will be filtered out by the glass. This is also true for sunlight, just in case you were thinking you could provide natural sunlight to an indoor turtle tank by locating the tank next to a window. This doesn't work. Plus, doing so could make the tank too hot.

There is another kind of light called a mercury vapor bulb. This provides both heat and full-spectrum lighting. While you're looking at lights at the store, check them out, too. They can be more expensive than other lights, but they may cut down the number of lights you'll actually need.

You can use timers, available at stores that sell electrical supplies, to automatically turn the lights on and off, to simulate day/night cycles for your turtles.

UVB fluorescent lighting fixtures are a must when keeping chelonians.

Electronic timers can be used with lights and heating devices.

Temperature

Use thermometers to keep track of the temperatures on both the land area and in the water. For most pet aquatic turtles, overall temperatures from 75°F to 79°F (24°C to 26°C) should be OK. As mentioned, however, you should provide a warm spot for basking; this can go up to 89°F (32°C).

Keep the water temperature at around 75°F (24°C). If you keep your turtle tank in a basement or other cool area, there are heating products such as infrared devices, heat pads, and heat tapes available that allow you to raise the temperature inside the tank. Lighting, of course, helps raise the temperature, too. Always remember to use caution when using electrical components around water.

At night you can use colored light bulbs, such as red bulbs, to heat the enclosure, or non-light-emitting products such as those described above. The nighttime temperature doesn't have to be as warm as the daytime temperature; lowering the temperature to around 67°F (19°C) is normally OK.

Other Housing Options

Turtles can be kept in various other containers, including watering troughs such as those used by horses; metal tubs; bins; and large plastic containers (including some of the popular Rubbermaid brands or pools specifically made for aquatic turtles). The key is to always be sure the containers can provide the environment your pets need—including a good amount of space and decent air circulation (something aquariums may be lacking)—and can accommodate the equipment (lights and so on) you will need to care for your pets.

Set Up an Outdoor Turtle Pool

You know those plastic kiddie wading pools? They can be used to create a nice outdoor enclosure for aquatic turtles. Adults should supervise younger children in constructing the following enclosure. Here's what you'll need to set one up:

 A plastic wading pool, available at toy stores, and lawn and garden stores

 Stackable rocks, including smooth rocks and flat rocks (slate), which you can find outdoors and at building supply and some tropical fish supply stores

 A board to place over the top of a portion of the pool to provide shade

 A screen covering

 Wooden two-by-twos to make a frame for the screen cover

 Screws and washers to attach screening to the wooden frame

 Silicone sealant (available at tropical fish supply stores and hardware stores)

Simply stack rocks in the middle of the pool and add water. Use the same water conditioners recommended in the aquatic turtle housing section to treat the water. Stack the rocks in such a way that the turtles in your pond can't knock them down and hurt themselves. You can build one or two land areas, perhaps in the middle of the pool, that would allow space for a couple of turtles or for one larger one to bask. Remember to arrange the land area so the turtles can get all the way out of the water to dry off. Flat pieces of slate make nice basking areas. Just be sure the edges aren't sharp enough to hurt your pets. Sealing the rocks together with silicone can help prevent injury.

Outdoor enclosures are great for both turtles and tortoises because sunlight goes a long way toward keeping them in tip-top  health. Even so, provide some shady areas over your pool so the turtles can get out of the sun if they want. You can do this by locating the pool near a tree or a bush that provides partial shade or by covering a portion of the top opening with one or two boards. Just be sure you don't cover it up so much that no sun can get to your turtles!

Place screening over the top of the pool to keep out cats and other predators that may be roaming your neighborhood. This will also keep your turtles in; turtles can climb better than  you may think. Attach screening firmly and securely all the way around the top of the pool by using the two-by-twos to build a wooden frame sized to cover the top of the entire pool. Then stretch and attach the screening to the frame using the screws and washers.

Inside the pool, arrange some rocks and slate to provide hiding places for your turtles. They need these to feel safe. Again, arrange rocks securely so they don't fall down on top of your turtles. The boards across the top of the pool will provide security as well as shade.

CHAPTER 5

Making a Good Tortoise Home

I n this chapter, you'll learn how to make a proper home for tortoises. Tortoises do best when kept outside. They need a lot of space and access to sunlight to really thrive. If you must keep a tortoise indoors, the best enclosure for it is a tortoise table. See the activity in this chapter for instructions on how to build one.

Galapagos tortoise

An Outdoor Tortoise Pen

It isn't recommended that a young tortoise keeper attempt to construct a tortoise pen alone. Get someone, such as an adult or older relative, who has at least a little knowledge about building to help you. This person should be able to read the following basic details and use them as a jumping-off point to build the perfect outdoor tortoise pen.

An outdoor tortoise pen needs walls to keep the tortoise inside. These can be made of

Texas tortoise

various materials, depending on how large and how strong the tortoise is (and how hard it can push against the wall should it decide to do so). Some common materials are logs, boards, and concrete blocks. You may need to use mortar to make block walls firm, and boards may need to be nailed or screwed to fence posts or two-by-fours.

The tortoise pen can be freestanding, or it can be located against your house or an existing wall to cut down the amount of wall construction necessary to form the pen.

Walls can be sunk into the

Be sure any grass in a tortoise pen is not treated with pesticides.

African spurred tortoises

Mesh on the bottom of the pen will prevent burrowing.

ground and arranged to form a rectangle or square enclosure. Digging a trench first, a couple of feet deep, and sinking the walls into the trench will help prevent a tortoise from digging its way out of the pen. Tortoises need a lot of room to roam, and pens measuring about 12 feet (4 meters) long by 10 feet (3 meters) wide and larger are not out of the ordinary. Do your research, know how large your tortoise will grow, and size its pen accordingly.

Some people build covers for their tortoise pens. This helps keep predatory animals, such as cats, raccoons, and dogs, out of them. The covers can also keep tortoises, some of which can climb, in. Covers can be constructed by building wooden frames with screening stretched over them, with as many of these sections as needed to cover the pen. Depending on the size of the pen, it may be one large cover or several smaller ones.

Shady areas should be available in outdoor pens. These can be created by locating the pen next to a tree or a bush that will provide shade or by constructing roofed shelters to provide shade (basically, a roof on top of some posts, beneath which tortoises can sit).

Note: A wading pool setup such as the one described in chapter 4 can also be used to house tortoises outside. Instead of water, place straw or clean soil inside it. Again, provide shady areas and hiding places, and be sure the pets you plan to keep in it can't climb out.

Pen covers keep tortoises in and predators out of tortoise enclosures.

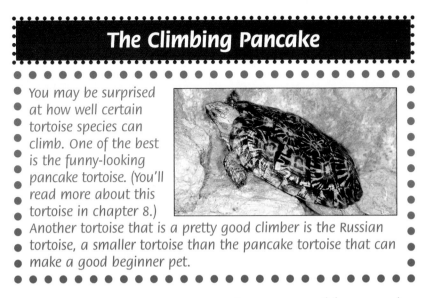

You may be surprised at how well certain tortoise species can climb. One of the best is the funny-looking pancake tortoise. (You'll read more about this tortoise in chapter 8.) Another tortoise that is a pretty good climber is the Russian tortoise, a smaller tortoise than the pancake tortoise that can make a good beginner pet.

Inside the Pen

It's best to provide different types of substrate, or ground, in the pen. The pen should contain some growing grass because tortoises like to graze on grass. It's healthy for them to eat; just be sure the grass has never been treated with fertilizers or pesticides. The ground does not need to be completely covered with grass. Scrubby areas with plants should be in the pen as well. Learn about your tortoise's natural habitat, and do your best to copy that habitat in your own pen.

Inside the pen, your tortoise needs a house to go to for security, to get out of the sun, and to sleep. Some tortoise keepers use small doghouses or open-ended wooden boxes for this purpose. Heavy plastic containers turned upside down with a hole cut into one side can be used, too. If you choose a tortoise house with a floor, it can be raised off the ground so it stays dry inside

Rocks that are used in the pen must be secured in place for tortoise safety.

if it rains. It can be placed on a wooden or metal frame, or it can be placed on top of some bricks. If you go this route, you'll need to add a ramp that's wide enough to allow your tortoise to crawl into the shelter easily. You don't expect your pet to pole-vault into its house, do you? Place some hay inside the house to make it more comfy for your tortoise.

You can decorate an outdoor tortoise pen with plants, rocks, and other natural materials. It can be set up to resemble a little slice of nature. Just remember, though, that your tortoise may decide to do some redecorating of its own by

Don't let your pen become overcrowded, like this one. Crowding can lead to illness.

plowing through plants or pushing against rocks. Don't stack anything that could fall down on top of your pet should it push against that object.

For a water dish, sink a shallow plastic container into the ground so that its top is at ground level. The container doesn't have to be more than a few inches deep because the tortoise does not need to submerge itself entirely in this dish. It should be big enough for the entire tortoise to sit in, though. Your pet should be able to easily enter and exit this container. Your tortoise may drink the

Always check that your pen is escape proof. Some tortoises can climb fairly well.

water or simply soak in it. Either way, the water should be replaced with fresh water at least a few times per week, even if the water looks as if it is clean. Food can be served on a large shallow pan placed on the ground.

These are the basics for what you need to think about when building your own outdoor tortoise pen. Keeping your tortoise outdoors gives it access to unfiltered sunlight and is one of the best things you could do for your pet.

Avoid Tortoise Fights

When you are planning your tortoise housing and the number of tortoises you intend to keep in an enclosure, be aware that keeping two adult  male tortoises together may lead to problems. If they can see each other frequently, they will likely fight, ramming each other and trying to flip each other over onto their backs.

Aggression will be less severe if the tortoises are housed in a very large outdoor pen that contains rocks, bushes, and other objects that prevent male tortoises from constantly seeing each other. Even so, don't be surprised if two or more males decide to mix it up. If this happens often enough, you will need to keep them in separate enclosures. Pairs (a male and female) that are kept together may be less grumpy toward each other, and they may even mate (although this can involve mating behavior during which the male may pursue and knock against the female). Multiple females are less likely to exhibit any aggression.

Build an
Indoor
Tortoise Table

Sometimes people can't keep their pet tortoises outside. Maybe they live in apartments or small houses without enough yard space for an outdoor tortoise pen. For anyone who can't keep a tortoise outdoors, an indoor tortoise table is the best way to go

Beginners should get someone, such as an adult or older relative who knows how to build things, to help them construct a tortoise table. Young children should not attempt this project alone. Basic details are provided here, but a knowledgeable person should still be involved. It's also a lot easier to build with other people helping.

To build a tortoise table measuring 4 feet by 8 feet (a recommended size for several tortoises), you'll need the following materials:

☑ For the longer walls: two plywood or melamine boards measuring 8 feet long by 1 inch thick. The width of the boards is the height of the walls of the finished table, and the size depends on how big your tortoise will be. You want the walls at least twice as tall as the tortoises. Eighteen- to 24-inch-tall walls usually work well.

☑ For the shorter walls: two plywood or melamine boards measuring 4 feet 2 inches long by 1 inch thick. The width should be the same as that of the longer walls.

☑ For the bottom: a sheet of plywood or melamine measuring 8 feet long by 4 feet wide

☑ For assembling: stainless steel brackets, fasteners, and screws to attach the walls to each other and to the floor

☑ For sealing: silicone sealant (you can get it in aquarium, pet, or hardware stores)

✅ For finishing: waterproof finish (available at hardware and do-it-yourself stores) if plywood is used.

Once you have all the necessary materials and tools (hammer, screwdriver, brush), follow the steps below to construct your pen.

1. Lay the floor board down, and position one of the longer side walls along it, standing the wall up on its edge. Secure the bottom of the wall to the edge of the floor board using some screws, spaced about 12 inches apart.

2. Once you have one of the longer walls attached, do the same with the other long wall.

3. Now position one of the shorter walls across one of the open ends, butting it up against the edges of both the floor board and the two longer walls.

Screw this wall to the edges of the floor board and both of the longer walls. Use L-shaped brackets to attach the shorter and longer walls to each other as well.

4. Do the same thing with the remaining shorter wall, and you will have the basic tortoise table formed.

5. With all screws and brackets firmly in place, use silicone sealant to seal the seams inside the table, where the walls and floor board are joined to each other. Sand any rough edges.

6. As a final step, coat the interior wood surfaces with a waterproofing finish (such as a polyurethane finish), which will help keep the wood in good shape.

Food and water bowls come in many shapes and sizes. Use containers that cannot be tipped over by your tortoises.

Possible substrates (what goes in the bottom) include manufactured substrates especially for tortoises and other reptiles, clean soil (which can be mixed with playground sand, available at building supply stores), cypress bark chips (available at stores that sell reptile supplies as well as nurseries), or timothy hay (often available at pet stores that sell supplies for rabbits and guinea pigs, as well as feed stores that sell supplies for horses). The substrate should be deep enough in areas to allow burrowing. Place a shallow water pan in the bottom of the enclosure, then fill the bottom

of the tortoise table with substrate until it reaches the top edge of the water pan. It does not have to be too deep, as the water pan itself doesn't have to be very deep—a couple of inches is enough. The pan should be large enough to allow a tortoise to fit its entire body inside. Watch for water spilling out of the water pan and soaking the substrate. This can lead to mold and possible fungal infections. Replace any damp substrate as necessary.

Include a hide box for tortoises kept in the tortoise table. Tortoises may group together in one hide box, so the size of the box should depend on how many tortoises live in the enclosure. You can also supply more than one hide box if necessary. A hide box is basically a box with one end that's open so the tortoise can crawl in and out. Hide boxes make sturdy retreats where a tortoise can feel safe. They can be made of wooden or plastic boxes turned upside down on top of the substrate, with one "wall" removed. Obviously, the hide box should be large enough to allow tortoises to easily enter and exit.

When feeding tortoises in a tortoise table, place a food tray on top of the substrate. This keeps your pet from accidentally eating any substrate along with its food, which could lead to health problems.

Use full-spectrum lighting over the entire tortoise table, and a basking light at one end, just as you would provide for aquatic turtles. (These lights are described in the previous chapter). If you have other household pets, such as cats, consider constructing a wood-framed, screened top for the tortoise table. You can place any lighting fixtures on top of this cover.

Aquariums for Hatchling Tortoises

Hatchling (recently hatched) tortoises are often available for sale, and they can be kept in an aquarium as small as 10 gallons (38 L), but they will quickly outgrow this enclosure and need to be moved to a tortoise table or an outdoor pen.

The bottom of the tortoise aquarium can contain timothy hay, cypress bark chips, or clean soil, sometimes mixed with

Get Them Outside

If you keep pet tortoises inside, try to get them outside several times a week so they can benefit from some direct sunlight. Take them out, and let them walk around under your supervision. A backyard or back patio works fine. Be wary about taking them out in public places, however, where they could come in contact with dogs and other possible threats. And always keep an eye on them.

Cypress mulch is an attractive natural substrate.

playground sand (available at building supply stores). Although alfalfa pellets—the same kind you feed pet rabbits—are often used as bottom material, beware of using them for your aquarium. Your tortoises may eat them, and if the pellets become moist, they can quickly become moldy. Both situations can lead to possible health problems.

Provide full-spectrum lighting, and add an overhead basking light at one end of the aquarium. (See the previous chapter for more info about these lights.) A hide box should be provided, too. (See "Build an Indoor Tortoise Table" for a description of a hide box.) Some people place the basking light over the hide box to heat the inside of the hiding place.

Do your research about any tortoise you want to keep. Knowing about its natural habitat will guide you in supplying the proper temperature and humidity levels in the aquarium (or any tortoise enclosure). Use thermometers in the aquarium to keep track of temperature levels, and read the hints for providing humidity in the section in chapter 8 on the red-footed tortoise.

Other Housing Options

Tortoises can be kept in various other containers, including watering troughs such as those used by horses, metal tubs, and

This is a baby red-footed tortoise. Learn what kind of enclosure best suits your pet.

bins. You can also set tortoises up in plastic wading pools such as those described in the previous chapter. Just add a substrate for tortoises rather than water as

Tubs can be used for both tortoises and aquatic turtles. This one has a ramp that turtles can climb to go from water (below) to land (top).

recommended for aquatic turtles. The key is to always be sure the containers can provide the elements your pets need—including a good amount of space, decent air circulation (something aquariums don't always provide), and hiding places—and can accommodate the equipment (lights and so on) you will need to care for your pets.

OK, you now know the basics of what's involved to properly house healthy pet turtles and tortoises. In the following chapter, we'll look at what kind of food you should feed your new pets.

CHAPTER 6

Chelonian Chow

Feeding turtles and tortoises is not too complicated, but there are some important guidelines. Variety always plays an important part of any pet reptile's diet. Try to offer as many of these foods as you can, rather than feeding the same food day in and day out. That gets boring for your pet. Even if your pets do actively gulp down the same food meal after meal (and they probably would), still vary their menu items. It makes it more interesting for both keeper and the kept, and offering different foods could renew your pet's interest in eating if it stopped eating the items you were offering previously.

Eastern box turtle

Tortoises like to graze on grass and healthy, calcium-rich greens.

Food for Turtles

You don't need to feed your turtles every day. Feeding them three or four times a week is fine. All the aquatic turtles mentioned in the "Excellent Turtles for Beginners" section of chapter 7 should accept some or all of the following foods:

- commercially manufactured turtle foods, such as pellets, sinking tablets, and sticks
- cooked chicken
- earthworms and other insects, such as mealworms
- lean raw beef (sparingly)
- live aquatic plants sold for fish tanks
- live guppies
- live small feeder goldfish
- minced beef heart (sparingly; buy in grocery stores and mince in blender)
- trout chow
- vegetables such as romaine lettuce, zucchini, and carrots

Commercially manufactured turtle foods are an excellent primary food for aquatic turtles. They are prepared with turtle nutrition in mind and will help you maintain healthy turtles by providing necessary nutrients. Some of these foods sink, others float (all aquatic turtles eat in the water). Try different types, and see which ones your turtles prefer.

Turtles are carnivores, meaning they eat meat (including worms).

I get tired of the same old worms every day!

Remember: variety is important. How would you like to eat the same old worms every day? Don't overfeed, either. Turtles are often voracious and will eat whatever you put in front of them. Consult with the person who sold you your turtle about the proper amounts of food for your pet.

Special-Needs Turtles

Map turtles (read more about maps in chapter 7) may eat some of the foods listed on page 67, but they should also be offered snails (you can buy some at tropical fish stores), crayfish, freshwater shrimp, and insects. Because of these special feeding requirements, map turtles can be a bit more difficult to keep in captivity than other turtles are.

Box turtles (read more about them in chapter 7) eat some of the foods from the list, including earthworms, mealworms, cooked chicken, raw beef, vegetables, and commercial box turtle foods. You can also offer them slugs, snails, and tiny "pinkie" mice (hairless newborn baby mice). They eat fruit that can be found on the tortoise food list on page 69 as well.

Map turtle

Feeding tortoises is simple because they're vegetarians that eat easy-to-find food.

Food for Tortoises

Tortoises are primarily vegetarian. They do fine if fed four times a week. The bulk of the diet of most of the species mentioned in the "Excellent Tortoises for Beginners" section of chapter 8 should consist of vegetation, including salads made from the following:

- dark, leafy greens, including collard, mustard, and dandelion
- flowers, including hibiscus, roses, and carnations
- hay, both timothy and alfalfa
- high-fiber grasses and weeds
- vegetables, both fresh and frozen (thaw them first), including peas, carrots, squashes, zucchini, green beans, and lima beans

If you keep tortoises indoors, pick some high-fiber grasses and weeds for them, or take them outdoors and let them graze while keeping an eye on them. Be sure you don't offer them any grasses or weeds

Dining Out

Feed your aquatic turtles in a separate container instead of in their home tank. By doing so, you will help keep their home tank cleaner. You'll still need to change the water and otherwise maintain a clean turtle tank, but feeding aquatic turtles in a separate container does help a lot with cleanliness.

Unlike most tortoises, red-foots can be given small amounts of protein.

Cooked egg (including the shell) can also be offered. Don't overdo the protein; remember that only a small amount is necessary. However, don't feed tortoises that are primarily herbivorous protein, or they could suffer from gout and possibly pyramiding (see chapter 9).

that have been sprayed with pesticides or fertilizers.

Red-footed tortoises (read more about them in chapter 8) eat much the same vegetarian diet as other tortoises do, but a small portion of their diet should be protein-rich foods. Protein can be supplied about once a week by feeding some dry low-fat cat or dog food that is soaked in water until it's soft.

A small amount of fruits can be offered to tortoises. Types to mix into their veggie salad on occasion include:

- apples
- bananas
- blueberries
- grapes
- mangoes
- melons (including cantaloupe, honeydew, watermelon)
- raspberries
- strawberries

Hungry tortoises are usually healthy tortoises, and it's fun to watch a group of them enthusiastically chowing down on their salads.

Calcium Supplements

Supplemental calcium is important when keeping chelonians. For turtles, you (or an adult) can chop up pieces of cuttlebone (sold for birds in pet stores) and leave them to float in the turtle tank, where turtles may nibble on them. Aquatic turtles may also gnaw on calcium blocks you can purchase at pet and tropical fish stores.

Tortoises and box turtles can receive supplemental calcium in the form of powder sprinkled on their food, both living and not. This can be calcium powder you buy in the reptile section of a pet store, or it can be shaved cuttlebone.

CHAPTER 7

Turtles Are Terrific!

All the turtles that are mentioned in this chapter are aquatic, except for one: the box turtle. First, we'll look at some common turtles that are kept as pets. Then, we'll look at a few other aquatic turtles that are interesting in their own right, even though they are not recommended as pets for beginners.

Red-eared turtles

Excellent Turtles for Beginners

There are six primary types of turtles I recommend for beginners:

1. common musk turtle
2. map turtles
3. mud turtles
4. painted turtles
5. red-eared slider
6. Reeve's turtle

There are seven, if you include box turtles. Because of the problems facing wild populations (see "Don't Take Box Turtles" on page 25), I recommend only captive-bred box turtles. Any of these species can make a hardy pet if you provide the proper care in the form of a large enough, clean enclosure with the proper food, lighting, temperature, and so on.

Musk turtles are hardy pets, even if they are kind of ugly.

Common Musk Turtles

The common musk turtle (*Sternotherus odoratus*) is called the stinkpot. With words such as *musk*, *odor*, and *stink* used to describe it, you may think this is one smelly turtle. Well, sometimes it is. The common musk turtle can emit a stinky musk from two pairs of glands located on each side of its body. In the United States, wild musk turtles can be found from Maine south to Florida and west to the Great Lakes region and Texas.

The common musk's shell is more highly domed than that of the flatter aquatic turtle. Its plastron is different, too, being much narrower. This is not a very pretty turtle. It is mostly grayish and brownish, with a light-colored stripe near each eye and a somewhat pointy nose. It has a bulbous head, and its neck skin looks like it has goose bumps. The common musk can also be a bit snappy and may try to bite you if it's annoyed.

The common musk turtle may not sound like a good pet, but because it is readily available; fairly small, with adults measuring about 4 inches (10 cm); and usually very hardy and easy to care for, it can make a good pet. Its weird-looking features even have their own charm. The musk turtle is not an active swimmer like the other turtles mentioned in this section. It swims a little, but chances are you'll often see it walking on the bottom of the tank rather than actively swimming. Musks also don't bask as often as the other species,

Musk turtle but a basking spot should still be provided.

Because the common musk turtle is not as large as the other species mentioned in this section, a 30-gallon (114-L) aquarium is fine for two adult turtles. Keep them at room temperature, 73°F to 79°F (23°C to 26°C), with an area that is 80°F to 88°F (27°C to 31°C) beneath the basking bulb over the haul-out area.

Map Turtles

Map turtles (*Graptemys* spp.) come by their common name because of the fine lines—which look like the lines you would find on a map—that cover their shells. The carapaces of map turtles have a raised saw-tooth-shaped structure, the **keel**, that runs down the middle. For this reason, some map turtles, especially the ones with more prominent keels, are also known as sawbacks. These turtles have a wide range and can be found in, among other states, Alabama, the Dakotas, Florida, Illinois, Indiana, Minnesota, Ohio, and Texas.

For the most part, map turtles are tan in color, with varying degrees of yellow, pale orange, and darker highlights. Female

Map turtles do well in enclosures that feature moving water.

maps can grow up to about 12 inches (30 centimeters) in carapace length. Males, by contrast, grow to only about 5 inches (13 cm) or so. For this reason, if you want to keep map turtles, you may want to consider keeping males because they're smaller.

The temperatures mentioned for keeping common musk turtles is OK for maps. Map turtles prefer swimming in rivers, though, rather than in ponds and lakes. Therefore, if you want to keep a map turtle, you need to provide some movement in the water section of its tank. This can be done by using a powerhead, which you can buy in pet and tropical fish stores. When placed in the water and turned on, the powerhead shoots out a jet of water, creating a current. Don't use a powerhead that's too powerful, though—you don't want it to shove your turtle all over the tank. Read the instructions so you can create a steady current but not a super-strong one.

Map turtles are more difficult to keep than other species such as red-eared sliders and painted turtles because of their special requirements for water movement and food (see chapter 6). Beginners may want to gain some experience keeping some of the other species mentioned in this section before trying their luck with maps.

Map turtle

Box turtles are good species for beginners. However, the number of wild box turtles in the southwestern, central, and eastern United States has dropped very low. Don't buy any box turtles unless you know that they are captive-bred.

Their care requirements are different from those of the other pet turtles mentioned in this chapter. Box turtles, which average 5 to 6 inches (13 to 15 centimeters) in length, are not aquatic, so they don't need a water area as the others do. They are more woodsy, and a couple can be kept in a 60-gallon (227-L) aquarium on small orchid bark chips mixed with potting soil. (A single box turtle can be kept in a 20-gallon [76-L] aquarium.) Provide a hide box into which your turtles can enter and exit easily.

Box turtles like humidity, which is one reason an aquarium is OK for them. Aquariums contain humidity quite well. Place a basking light at one end of the enclosure, with a hot spot 84°F to 89°F (29°C to 32°C). The other end of the cage should be cooler, 75°F to 79°F (24°C to 26°C). Provide full-spectrum lighting, too (see chapter 4).

Other types of enclosures, including a tortoise table, can work for box turtles. See chapter 5 for instructions about building a tortoise table and chapter 4 for some other housing ideas, including an outdoor enclosure using a plastic wading pool, that could work for box turtles.

Mud turtles are small, like musk turtles, making them good "starter turtles."

Mud Turtles

Mud turtles (*Kinosternon* spp.) are other aquatic turtles that can be good pets because they are small and hardy. Adults average about 5 inches (13 cm) in length. As with the common musk turtle, two adults of most mud turtle species can usually be kept comfortably in a 30-gallon (114-L) aquarium. Like the common musk turtle, mud turtles are not known for basking, but they should still have a basking site in their enclosure.

Wild mud turtles can be found throughout the southern and central areas of the United States, extending north to New England. Temperatures for captive specimens are the same as suggested for the common musk turtle.

Painted Turtles

There are four subspecies of painted turtles: the eastern (*Chrysemys picta picta*), the western (*Chrysemys picta belli*), the midland (*Chrysemys picta marginata*), and the southern (*Chrysemys picta dorsalis*). The painted turtle has a huge range, and painted turtles of one type or another can be found across the United States.

Painted turtles exhibit beautiful colors, increasing their appeal to hobbyists.

Once you see a painted turtle, you will know why it comes by its common name. They are pretty, with shells exhibiting yellow, orange, red, and olive coloration. The skin is dark olive with yellow and sometimes reddish striping. Painted turtles are large–up to about 10 in (25 centimeters [cm])–and need plenty of swimming space in their tanks. Temperatures should range from 73°F (23°C) to 89°F (32°C), with the higher temperature being beneath a basking light.

No Painting!

Although nature has "painted" the shells of certain turtles with brilliant colors, you should never do so yourself. The chemicals in paint can seriously harm your pets, and the paint can cause their shells to become deformed.

Red-Eared Slider

The red-eared slider (*Trachemys scripta elegans*) is the most popular pet aquatic turtle of all time.

It is called red-eared because of the red mark on both sides of its head. The skin is green with yellow stripes, and the carapace is dark green (it can turn almost black in older turtles). The plastron is yellow with dark blotches. There are also different colored morphs of the red-eared for sale, such as pastel and albino red-eared sliders. These interesting types cost more than the normal green and yellow red-eared.

This is the turtle that often ended up in the plastic turtle bowl with a palm tree setup described in chapter 4. It is now bred by the millions at commercial turtle farms.

There was a huge demand for red-eared sliders after the Teenage Mutant Ninja Turtles showed up back in the 1980s. This was unfortunate for the many turtles that were bought on impulse. Ninja Turtle fans wanted their own turtle pets without really knowing how to keep them alive, and turtles died as a result.

Red-eared sliders can get big; adults grow to about 10 inches (25 cm) in length. They need basking areas and a lot of

The red-eared slider has been a very popular pet since the early days of herp keeping.

What's a Morph?

Morphs are groups of animals within a species that have characteristics—usually color or pattern—that are different from those of "normal" individuals of the same species. One example would be an albino red-eared slider, which is a different color (yellow with red eyes) than a typical red-eared slider, which is green. Turtle breeders try breeding morphs together to create larger numbers of these unique turtles, which cost more than the "normal" types of the same species.

swimming room in their tanks, as described in chapter 4. They can be kept in the same temperature ranges as those provided for painted turtles. For people who can provide the right kind of environment, red-eared sliders are wonderful, personable turtle pets.

Wild red-eared sliders originally inhabited the Mississippi Valley, from Illinois to the Gulf of Mexico, but this turtle has spread

in the United States and can now be found in many other states.

Reeve's Turtles

All the previously mentioned species live in the United States. The Reeve's turtle (*Chinemys reevesii*) lives in China and Japan. It's an attractive smaller turtle (5 inches [13 cm]) that exhibits varying coloration, including brownish or greenish gray and yellowish brown. Its head can have yellow stripes.

This is another turtle with a keeled carapace, but instead of having the single keel a map turtle has, the Reeve's turtle has

The Reeve's turtle has three ridges, or keels down its back.

three keels running down the back of its carapace. Another interesting feature of the Reeve's turtle is that it has a somewhat rectangular shell, as opposed to the more oval shells of the species mentioned previously.

Reeve's turtles become quite tame, doing well in the proper captive environment, and make good pets. Some people opt for these rather than sliders because they are smaller, usually 6 inches [15.25cm]. Temperatures for Reeve's turtles can be 73°F to 77°F (23°C to 25°C), with a basking area at 83°F to 89°F (28°C to 32°C).

Other Cool Turtles

Now you know about types of turtles that you could consider keeping as pets. Let's look at some other interesting aquatic turtles. I'm not recommending these for beginning turtle hobbyists, though, and that includes you!

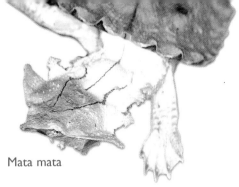

Mata mata

Mata Mata Turtles

The mata mata (*Chelus fimbriatus*) has a ridged and rough carapace, which helps it blend in with its underwater habitat. It lives in shallow, slow-moving water in South America, where it can be found moving along the muddy bottom.

The name *mata mata* means "kill, kill" and this turtle is good at doing just that to any fish or other aquatic animal that it wants to eat. The mata mata has

The mata mata is easily one of the oddest-looking turtles available today.

The Smiling Turtle

When you look head-on at a mata mata turtle, you may notice that it appears to be smiling back at you! Its mouth is just shaped that way.

a unique feeding behavior: it uses a vacuum! It remains perfectly still underwater, blending in with the surrounding area because of its rough-edged shell and the many jagged and rough edges of the skin on its head and legs. When a tasty fish swims within range, the mata mata suddenly shoots its head forward, opens its mouth, and sucks in a bunch of water, along with the fish! The turtle then spits out the water and swallows the fish whole.

This turtle is one of the more bizarre-looking ones you'll ever see. (You can see specimens in pet stores, at reptile shows, and in public aquariums and zoos.) Little bits of skin stick out all along its head and legs, and it has a long, pointy nose that it uses like a snorkel to breathe air.

The Snappers

There are two different species of snapping turtle. The smaller of the two is the common snapping turtle. Its scientific name is *Chelydra serpentina*, which it likely got because of its long, snaky (or *serpentine*, which means "snakelike") neck.

Snappers are meat eaters. Now pretend this worm is your finger.

The larger alligator snapper (*Macroclemys temminckii*) is the largest freshwater turtle in the United States. It lives in deep water in swamps, in rivers, and in other bodies of water in the southeastern United States, including Alabama, Florida, Louisiana, and Texas. This turtle can weigh about 200 pounds (91 kilograms)! The head of an adult alligator snapping turtle is so massive that it can't be pulled into its shell. Instead, the head remains outside the shell, surrounded by folds of flabby flesh. Maybe that's why this turtle has developed such a powerful bite over the years, a bite that could easily snap a stick in two or break your finger.

You may think this turtle gets its name because of its biting ability. But the name *alligator*

The Turtle That Stole a King's Sword

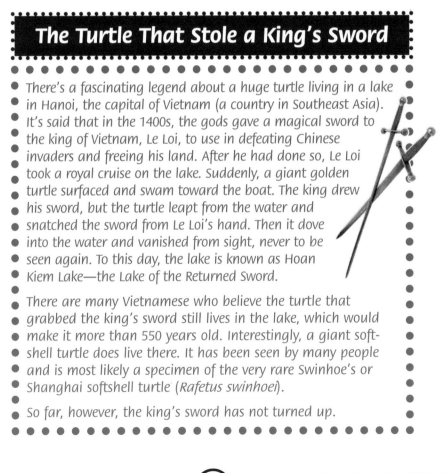

There's a fascinating legend about a huge turtle living in a lake in Hanoi, the capital of Vietnam (a country in Southeast Asia). It's said that in the 1400s, the gods gave a magical sword to the king of Vietnam, Le Loi, to use in defeating Chinese invaders and freeing his land. After he had done so, Le Loi took a royal cruise on the lake. Suddenly, a giant golden turtle surfaced and swam toward the boat. The king drew his sword, but the turtle leapt from the water and snatched the sword from Le Loi's hand. Then it dove into the water and vanished from sight, never to be seen again. To this day, the lake is known as Hoan Kiem Lake—the Lake of the Returned Sword.

There are many Vietnamese who believe the turtle that grabbed the king's sword still lives in the lake, which would make it more than 550 years old. Interestingly, a giant soft-shell turtle does live there. It has been seen by many people and is most likely a specimen of the very rare Swinhoe's or Shanghai softshell turtle (*Rafetus swinhoei*).

So far, however, the king's sword has not turned up.

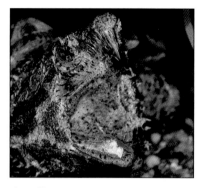

The alligator snapper uses a built-in lure to attract fish to its waiting mouth.

comes from its unusual carapace, which features three thick alligator-like keels that extend down its back. This is one tough turtle!

When hunting for food underwater (where it spends most of its time), the alligator snapper does something very interesting. It uses a "lure" to catch fish to eat. This lure is a piece of red flesh in the turtle's mouth that it wriggles so it looks like a live worm. The snapper remains still under the water, with its mouth wide open and its lure wriggling, until a fish notices the "worm" and swims over to investigate. Then—WHAM!—the snapper chomps down on its dinner.

The common snapper does not use a lure. Instead, it relies on stealth and speed. When one is after fish or other prey, it can be very quick. Both snappers are dark colored, which helps conceal them from their potential meals-to-be.

SoftShell Turtles

You can tell by their common name what softshell turtles are known for—a shell that is soft. Their shells are covered by a leathery skin instead of hard scutes, and softshell turtles are flat, too. They look like pancakes with a head and feet. They have tube-shaped noses that stick out and are used like snorkels to breathe air. This type of nose helps a turtle breathe while most of the turtle's body remains hidden beneath the water's surface, where it's less likely to attract unwanted attention from predators. Softshell turtles also are known for burying themselves in the bottom of

Softshell turtles have snorkel-like noses. This is a spiny softshell.

Softshells like to bury themselves in the sand. Three species live in the United States.

the bodies of water they inhabit. There they wait for fish and other aquatic animals to wander by so they can eat them.

There are three species that live in the United States. They are the Florida softshell (*Apalone ferox*), the spiny softshell (*Apalone spinifera*), and the smooth softshell (*Apalone mutica*).

There are other softshell turtles in Asia and Africa. One genus, *Chitra*, is especially interesting. Turtles in this genus are the narrow-headed softshell turtles. Compared with the rest of their large bodies, their heads look very small, giving them a bizarre appearance. These softshell turtles can get big, too. The alligator snapping turtle may be the biggest turtle in the United States, but the striped narrow-headed softshell turtle

(*Chitra chitra*) is likely the largest freshwater turtle species in the world. It can grow to lengths of about 4 feet (1 meter). Sadly, it is another fascinating turtle species that is critically endangered. (See chapter 10 for information about endangered species.)

Softshell turtles can make interesting pets. They need an aquatic setup but don't use regular aquarium gravel in the bottom of their tanks because the turtles could be hurt while trying to bury themselves in the gravel. Sand is recommended instead. These turtles are not for beginners. Among other reasons, they have a tendency to bite.

OK, we've discussed some cool turtles, both pets and otherwise. Now let's take a look at everybody's favorite land-dwelling chelonians, the tortoises.

CHAPTER 8

Time to Talk Tortoises

I am going to start this chapter by introducing tortoises that could make good pets for beginners, and I'll provide brief descriptions of each. These are meant to start you off—as I've said many times in this book, you should always do plenty of research before buying any reptile pet. Remember, too, to buy captive-bred tortoises whenever possible.

In the second part of the chapter, I'll talk about some other cool tortoises. Even though none of them is recommended for first-time tortoise keepers, they are fun to learn about.

Red-footed tortoise

Excellent Tortoises for Beginners

There are six tortoise species I recommend for new tortoise keepers. They are easier to keep than other tortoises are and don't grow too large. These are:

1. Greek tortoise
2. Hermann's tortoise
3. leopard tortoise
4. pancake tortoise
5. red-footed tortoise
6. Russian tortoise

Greek Tortoise

This attractive tortoise reaches a length of about 7 inches (18 cm). The Greek tortoise (*Testudo graeca*) is a normally hardy species that originally came from areas in the Middle East, Spain, Eastern Europe, and Africa. It exhibits different colors, includ-

The Greek tortoise is a smaller species.

ing brownish and olive, but there is also a "golden Greek" color variation that is yellow.

Temperatures for Greek tortoises can range from 79°F (26°C) to 89°F (32°C).

Hermann's tortoise

Hermann's Tortoise

The Hermann's tortoise (*Testudo hermanni*) resembles the Greek tortoise and has a good reputation as an excellent pet. Many are bred in captivity, so captive-bred specimens are readily available. This species has a reputation for being one of the more intelligent tortoises, and they can learn to recognize their owners (as sources of food, if nothing else).

Adult Hermann's tortoises can grow to about 10 inches (25 cm). The tortoise is native to southern Europe, and pets can be kept in enclosures with the temperature ranging from 73°F to 99°F (23°C to 37°C).

Leopard Tortoise

The leopard tortoise (*Geochelone pardalis*) is a hardy, medium-size tortoise. An adult can be about 20 inches (0.5 meter) long and can weigh up to about 32 pounds (15 kilograms) or so. It comes from Africa and is a beautiful tortoise with a high-domed shell. The black pattern on the pale yellow shell makes it a favorite among tortoise keepers.

Leopard tortoises can be kept in an indoor tortoise table, but a large outdoor pen will allow your tortoise to graze nat-urally. It might dig a bit, but this tortoise isn't as furious a burrow-er as, for instance, an African spurred tortoise (read about that species in "The Biggies" section). Leopard tortoises should be kept in dry conditions at temperatures between 80°F and 90°F (27°C and 32°C).

Pancake Tortoise

Most tortoises have dome-shaped carapaces. The pancake tortoise (*Malacochersus tornieri*) is an exception. The species' common name, besides perhaps making you hungry, gives a good idea of the shape of this tortoise's body—it's flat, maybe not quite as flat as a pancake, but very flat compared with other tortoises. The flat body allows

Leopard tortoise hatchlings can often be found for sale. They're cute aren't they?

Pancake tortoises are not widely bred in captivity and can be expensive.

the tortoise to crawl into tight cracks among the rocks that are found in its dry African habitat. To escape predators, it will squeeze into a really narrow place and use its front legs to wedge itself in tightly. A tucked-in pancake tortoise isn't coming out easily!

Pancake tortoises can make good pets, but captive-bred specimens can be somewhat expensive because they are not bred in large numbers in captivity. Still, try to buy a captive-bred one even though it may cost more.

The pancake tortoise is small, with adults reaching about 7 inches (18 cm). It is a good candidate for an indoor tortoise table. Rather than using a typical hide box, stack flat rocks in such a way as to provide gaps for the tortoises. Just be sure the rocks can't topple over and injure the tortoise. Consider using silicone sealant to attach the rocks to each other for stability. (Remember that young hobbyists should receive help from adults whenever silicone sealant is being used.) Remember that pancakes are good climbers.

Temperatures between 80°F and 89°F (27°C and 32°C) are OK for pancake tortoises during the day, and they can drop as low as 60°F (16°C) at night.

Pancake tortoise

Red-Footed Tortoise

The red-footed tortoise (*Geochelone carbonaria*) is pretty small, and it gets its name because of the red scales on its legs. It also has attractive red coloration on the head (some red-footed tortoises are called cherry heads). Adult males reach about 15 inches (38 cm) or so; females are a little smaller.

A hatchling red-foot takes a peek at the world while emerging from its egg.

These tortoises come from South America. The forests where they live are hot and humid, so you need to keep this in mind when maintaining them in captivity. You will need to provide a basking spot with temperatures from 93°F to 97°F (34°C to 36°C). Humidity can be provided by misting the tortoise's enclosure with water using a sprayer like that used on houseplants. You don't have to soak it until it's drenched—a light misting to moisten the environment and provide about 80 percent humidity is all that's needed.

Red-footed tortoise

A bark and soil substrate helps retain moisture and provide humidity, and humidity gauges that allow you to monitor the humidity level can be purchased at stores that sell reptile supplies.

A single hatchling can live in a 20-gallon (76-L) aquarium for a while, but eventually you will want to move it into a tortoise table or an outdoor pen. As with any pet tortoise's enclosure, be sure it is escape proof. The

walls should be at least twice as tall as any tortoise inside, and a little taller wouldn't hurt.

Although most tortoises should not be fed protein, the red-footed should. For more about feeding tortoises, including red-footed tortoises, see chapter 6.

Russian Tortoise

If you want a tortoise that does not get too big—a good trait in a pet for a beginner tortoise owner—the Russian tortoise, also known as Horsfield's tortoise (*Testudo horsfieldii*), is a

Hibernating Tortoises

Some pet tortoises, such as Russian tortoises, may benefit from being allowed to hibernate. Check with your reptile veterinarian for information about hibernation, whether a species you want to keep needs to hibernate, and the best way to allow it to do so, if necessary.

good choice. Generally, they top out at about 8 inches (20 cm) in length. Their color can vary somewhat, but most are olive or brown.

The Russian tortoise is also known as Horsfield's tortoise.

Handling Tortoises

Tortoises tolerate handling by their owners better than some other reptile pets that can be pretty squirmy. Hold the tortoise firmly so you don't accidentally drop it. Keep in mind that although a tortoise may not show signs that it is agitated while being held, the tortoise would probably prefer to be left alone. So don't overdo it with the handling.

Russian tortoises are burrowers, so if you keep them in an outside pen, be sure they can't burrow beneath the walls and escape. They are pretty good climbers, too. Any enclosure, then, whether an outside pen or a tortoise table, should be secure enough to prevent their escape. Provide a hide box for them, too, where they can feel secure.

The Russian tortoise can be found in Iran, northwestern China, Pakistan, Afghanistan, and Kazakhstan, where it lives in dry, rocky habitat. This species is more tolerant of temperature changes than some other tortoises. Pet Russian tortoises should be kept in dry conditions at temperatures between 75°F and 85°F (24°C and 29°C), with a basking spot of 90°F (32° C). Wild-caught Russian tortoises don't always fare well in captivity—as stated often in this book, captive-bred specimens are best.

Now you know six tortoise species that could make good pets for beginning tortoise keepers. In the following sections, we'll discover some other cool tortoises, even though none of them are recommended as beginner pets.

I'm a burrower but a pretty good climber, too!

Russian tortoise

The Biggies

Let's look at three tortoises that can get really, really big. And by big, I mean huge. The first is the Galapagos giant tortoise. This is an endangered species, and you won't be finding it in any pet stores or at any reptile expos. The other two—the Aldabra tortoise and the African spurred tortoise—are available for sale. The Aldabra would cost you many dollars, but the spurred tortoise isn't very expensive, and hatchlings of this species are often for sale in stores and at reptile expos. However, you need to know that the supercute little hatchlings you see being offered for sale will, if they're kept healthy, get very large and are capable of damaging a yard, including digging up entire underground sprinkler systems!

Galapagos Giant Tortoise

This tortoise is the granddaddy of all tortoises. There are records of male Galapagos tortoises that have weighed more than

Galapagos tortoises can weigh hundreds of pounds and live for many years.

700 pounds (318 kilograms)! They're also known as Galaps, and you may have seen some live specimens in a zoo.

The tortoise comes by its common name because it's from the Galapagos Islands. The Galapagos archipelago (an archipelago is an area of water that contains islands) is located

Galapagos tortoise

The Galap's thick skin helps the tortoise retain moisture.

about 600 miles (966 km) off Ecuador, in South America. There are thirteen main islands and many smaller ones.

Digging Deep

Chapter 5 suggested sinking tortoise pen walls fairly deep into the ground to help prevent tortoises from digging under them. Another preventive measure is to bury heavy wire screening down in the ground and curve it upward against the inside of the pen's walls. Tortoises can't dig through the screening.

The tortoises live on some of the islands, and you can take tours out to see them. People who like reptiles are especially fascinated by the Galapagos Islands because, in addition to the magnificent giant tortoises, there are marine iguanas and land iguanas living there.

Geochelone nigra is the giant tortoise's current scientific name, but it used to be *Geochelone elephantopus*. (Sometimes scientific names get changed when scientists learn something new about an animal that causes it to be categorized differently.) You should be able to guess what animal people had in mind when they gave the Galapagos tortoise its first scientific name. The Galapagos tortoise reminded them of an elephant because of its size and its skin, which still reminds some people (including me) of an elephant's wrinkly gray skin. As with other tortoises, the thick skin helps keep moisture inside the Galap's body. The Galap's legs and feet also resemble an elephant's.

Galapagos giant tortoises are endangered for several reasons. Unfortunately, some people like to eat the eggs of Galapagos tortoises. (See chapter 10 for other tortoises that are endangered because people like to eat them.) The islands are part of a national park, and the tortoises living there are protected by laws, but **poachers** (people who illegally

The Galapagos tortoise is an endangered species due to many factors.

Noisy Tortoises

Tortoises don't have a reputation for being very noisy, but they do make some noise. Don't be surprised if you hear them hissing, grunting, or making other such sounds. These sounds usually accompany some sort of action, such as a fight between males. Hissing is often the result of a frightened tortoise that's getting rid of some air to help it retreat into its shell.

kill or take wild animals) sneak onto the islands to steal tortoise eggs, and sometimes they kill the adult tortoises, too. Wild pigs and cats, as well as hawks and other predators, eat tortoise eggs and hatchling tortoises. Meanwhile, the tortoises have to compete with goats for vegetation. Actually, people are responsible for most of the tortoises' problems. They introduced pigs, cats, and goats to the Galapagos Islands. These predators and competitors are on the islands today only because people brought them there!

Luckily, conservation programs have been created to remove the animals that don't belong on the islands—bad news for pigs, cats, and goats, but great news for the tortoises!

When I think of a wise, old tortoise, the Galapagos tortoise is the animal that comes to mind. Galaps definitely can get very old, even older than 100 years. One of the oldest Galapagos tortoises was named Harriet and lived in the Australia Zoo. According to the zoo, Harriet was 176 years old when she passed away! The Galapagos giant tortoise is a CITES Appendix I species. (See the "Who Decides That an Animal Is Endangered?" box in chapter 10 to learn about **CITES**.)

Aldabra Tortoise

The Aldabra is another huge tortoise, and another that can get really old. You've just read about Harriet the Galapagos tortoise. Harriet's a young kid, though, when compared with an Aldabra tortoise named Adwaita, who lived in the Alipore Zoo in Calcutta, India. When Adwaita died in March 2006, the tortoise was reportedly 250 years old! Of course, when it comes to the ages of some of these tortoises, it may be impossible to know for sure if the animal is really that old or not.

Like the Galapagos giant tortoise, the Aldabra tortoise is named after the place it lives— the Aldabra Atoll, which is a group of small islands in the

One Aldabra tortoise may have lived 250 years! That's old, even for a tortoise!

Indian Ocean. Its scientific name is *Geochelone gigantea*, and it's easy to see why it's considered gigantic. This tortoise can be bigger than some Galapagos giant tortoises, with males weighing more than 650 pounds (294 kg). The Aldabra tortoise, like so many other tortoise species, faces problems in nature, including habitat destruction, which you will read about in chapter 10. It is a CITES Appendix II species.

African Spurred Tortoise

You will likely see African spurred tortoises for sale in pet stores and at reptile expos. Known also as the sulcata tortoise and the spur-thighed tortoise (though there is another tortoise that goes by that name too), this species is regularly bred in captivity. The hatchlings are so cute and reasonably priced that it's very tempting to bring one home for a pet. Before you do that, however, read the rest of this section.

The African spurred tortoise (*Geochelone sulcata*) comes from—guess where—

African spurred tortoises are powerful diggers that can damage property.

Africa! There, it moseys around its home range along the southern edge of the Sahara Desert. You might think it gets pretty hot there, and you're right. These tortoises avoid the hottest parts of the day by hiding in deep burrows that they dig in the ground.

African spurred tortoises are notorious burrowers. Their burrows can be as long as 10 feet (3m)! They are strong, too. Pet African spurred tortoises that are kept in a backyard can dig burrows so deep and so extensive that they can ruin sprinkler systems,

African spurred tortoise

walls, and pretty much whatever else you've got in the ground in your yard. Keeping them in outdoor pens is pretty much your only housing option with adult tortoises; because they grow so large, keeping them indoors is impractical. Be sure they're contained properly in a pen you've made especially for them.

The African spurred tortoise can grow to weigh about 200 pounds (91 kg) and can live up to 100 years. If you get one, there's a good chance it'll live longer than you! It is called the African spurred tortoise because of the enlarged scales on the front of its front legs that look like spurs. These aid the tortoise while it's digging burrows.

African spurred tortoises can be hardy and fun pets if they're kept properly. They need lots of space and should be kept outdoors in grassy pens where they can dig safely. They eat a variety of grasses, flowers, and weeds. Fruits and vegetables should be fed in very small amounts or not at all. For the people who can keep them the right way, African spurred tortoises can make very rewarding reptile pets that have some personality.

U.S. Tortoises

Most tortoises are found in places other than the United States, and there isn't much opportunity for you to find wild specimens while herping in the United States. There are three U.S. species, and they all belong to the genus *Gopherus*. That name should make you think of a gopher, a rodent that burrows into the ground. These tortoises do that, too. The three U.S. species are the

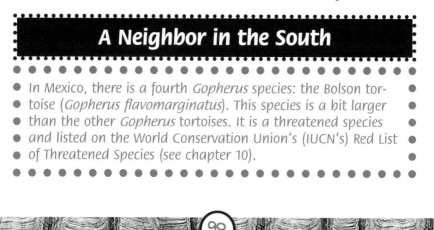

A Neighbor in the South

- In Mexico, there is a fourth *Gopherus* species: the Bolson tortoise (*Gopherus flavomarginatus*). This species is a bit larger than the other *Gopherus* tortoises. It is a threatened species and listed on the World Conservation Union's (IUCN's) Red List of Threatened Species (see chapter 10).

You can't buy or catch desert tortoises, but you can adopt them.

desert tortoise (*Gopherus agassizii*), the gopher tortoise (*G. polyphemus*), and the Texas tortoise (*G. berlandieri*).

All *Gopherus* tortoises have some level of government protection, meaning it's illegal to catch them and take them home, but you may find specimens available for adoption. Anyone keeping these tortoises needs to provide them with a yard or outdoor pen and access to plenty of sunlight. These grazing tortoises eat grasses, flowers (such as hibiscus and dandelions), and weeds. When you are offering plants such as these, be certain that they have not been sprayed with any pesticides. Greens, such as collard greens and dandelion greens, can be given in limited amounts. These tortoises need water, too, of course, and it can be provided in a shallow dish.

Desert Tortoise

The desert tortoise, *Gopherus agassizii* (named after scientist Louis Agassiz), is the western species, and it can be found in Arizona, California, Nevada, and Utah. This tortoise is currently experiencing problems with respiratory disease. (See "The Plight of the Desert Tortoise" in chapter 10.) Even though it is against the law to take desert tortoises out of the wild (they're protected because they're a **threatened** species, close to becoming endangered), people did for years, and some desert tortoise pets can still be found in the yards of residents in these western states.

This is a gopher tortoise burrow in south-central Florida.

There are also desert tortoise rescue-adoption centers. People who no longer want their tortoises take them to these centers. Sometimes people find tortoises on their property or tortoises that have been injured somewhere else, and they take them to the rescue centers, too.

Desert tortoise rescues often give the tortoises only to people who qualify. Before allowing someone to adopt a tortoise, a rescue center staff member may ask whether there is a pool in the yard and if so, if it is fenced (if it isn't, a tortoise could fall in and drown), and if the person owns a dog (which might want to chew on a tortoise). If you qualify, you can adopt a desert tortoise for a small fee and take home a cool pet that will live for years. Of course, don't plan to adopt a tortoise if you don't have a proper yard or pen in which to keep it, where it can roam around in the sunshine.

Because of the respiratory ailment that's affecting wild populations of desert tortoises, people who own them are asked not to release their pets into the wild. This appears to be how the wild tortoises got infected in the first place. You should never release a pet into the wild anyway. It not only could infect wild animals with a disease it may have picked up in captivity but also could be killed by other animals because it is not used to living in nature.

Gopher Tortoise

The gopher tortoise (*Gopherus polyphemus*) lives in sandy, scrubby areas of southwestern

and southeastern states, including Florida, Georgia, and Louisiana. It can grow to about 15 inches (38 cm) in length, and like so many chelonians, this one faces its share of troubles in the wild.

The biggest problem is all the houses, parking lots, stores, and other buildings and structures that keep getting built in its habitat. As a result, large numbers of gopher tortoises aren't just left homeless—they may get buried alive beneath the buildings! Because gopher tortoises dig deep burrows, some city governments have determined that the developers building on tortoise-inhabited land don't have to "waste" time and money digging them up. Many developers are allowed to build on top of the tortoises. In the various legal documents that approved this practice, it's called entombment. It's a sad situation, but the tortoises have people fighting for them, and this practice will be constantly under attack. Let's hope many gopher tortoises will be spared this fate. One solution is to move tortoises to protected land, where building construction won't occur. Who knows? Maybe by the time you're reading this book, there will be new laws in place to prevent gopher tortoises from being buried.

Texas Tortoise

Can you guess which state this tortoise lives in? *Gopherus berlandieri* also is experiencing decreasing habitat as—like everywhere else, it seems—more and more houses, shopping centers, and so on are built. As if that's not bad enough, a fair number of Texas tortoises get run over by cars, too. Again, these tortoises are protected by the government, but you can sometimes find them up for adoption.

This takes care of our tortoise section. Now let's learn about some potential health problems, what to do, and how to prevent them.

Texas tortoise

CHAPTER 9

Potential Health Problems

I t's always a bummer when pets get sick. Dealing with a sick turtle or tortoise is definitely something you want to avoid whenever possible, in large part because of the money you may have to spend to get your pet well. Of course, spending the necessary money when you have to is part of being a responsible pet owner.

Painted turtle

Chelonians may not show signs that they are sick until it's too late to save them.

Sometimes an animal may become ill through no fault of your own. For instance, it might be sick when you acquire it (chapter 3 provides hints about how to pick a healthy pet). But often, sad as it is to say, a pet turtle or tortoise becomes sick because of something its caretaker did wrong. It may not have been fed the right type of foods, or maybe it wasn't kept in the right kind of enclosure with proper lighting and at the correct temperature. Or perhaps warning signs of illness were ignored or not recognized.

In this chapter, we're going to look at some chelonian health considerations. *This information is not meant to be an in-depth examination into disease, and it is not meant to replace a visit to the veterinarian.* It is pre-sented to help you avoid certain conditions that could lead to your pet becoming sick and to aid in recognizing that something is wrong.

I always recommend that you take your pet to a vet at the first sign of illness, just to play it safe. For one thing, by the time a reptile, including a turtle or a tortoise, is showing signs of illness, it has likely already been sick for a while. In the wild, an animal that shows signs of illness is endangering its life. Illness is seen by other animals as being weak. A weak animal is easy prey, so animals hide their symptoms for as long as possible. Captive animals have retained this trait, so that by the time they do show signs of illness, there is no time to waste in making them well.

Fungal and bacterial infection can lead to respiratory disease in chelonians.

Respiratory Problems

A turtle or tortoise with a respiratory problem may wheeze and have trouble breathing. It may sneeze often or have a discharge or bubbles dribbling from its nose or eyes. The affected animal may breathe with its mouth open, may have no energy, and may stop eating. Its eyes may appear swollen.

Respiratory disease is very dangerous. A common cause, especially for a desert-dwelling tortoise, is an enclosure that is too cold or too damp. Yet another

Northern diamondback terrapin

reason to do your research first so you know what temperature is best for your pet! Respiratory problems can also result from fungal or bacterial infections.

If you notice the above symptoms in your pet turtle or tortoise, check the temperature of your pet's enclosure. Raise the temperature to 83°F to 87°F (28°C to 31°C) if necessary. If you have an aquatic turtle that's exhibiting any of these symptoms, in addition to checking the

Quarantine the Sick

If a sick animal is in an enclosure with other turtles or tortoises that appear healthy, quarantine it in a separate cage immediately. **Quarantine** means to keep the new animal isolated from any other pets until you're sure it is free from illness that it might otherwise pass on to your existing animals. Keep it warm, and make an appointment for your pet to be examined by a reptile-knowledgeable veterinarian.

air temperature of its enclosure, check the water temperature, as it may be too cold. Raising the overall enclosure temperature is usually a good idea and should be the first step toward making your pet well. After doing so, monitor your pet for a couple of days, watching closely for signs of improvement. If there are none, get to a veterinarian immediately, if not sooner.

Swollen or Crusted Eyes

Although respiratory disease can cause swollen eyes, it is not the only cause of this condition. A vitamin A deficiency is frequently the culprit, and you can

Take your pet to a vet if its eyes are swollen or otherwise abnormal.

supplement your pet's diet with vitamin A to help alleviate the problem. If the eyes appear to be crusted shut, try misting them lightly with warm water, or soak your pet in warm water, and see if it is then able to open its eyes. Of course, a consultation with your vet is still recommended.

Metabolic Bone Disease

Known also as nutritional secondary hyperparathyroidism, metabolic bone disease develops when a turtle or tortoise is fed an improper diet—one that is too low in calcium—and is not exposed to the proper full-spectrum lighting or sunlight. To boil it down to basics, your pet needs calcium for strong bones and shell. You can supply calcium by feeding calcium-rich foods, such as greens (dandelion, collard, and mustard), endive, bok choy, and Swiss chard, as well as calcium supplements, which are available in powdered form at pet stores. But this alone is not enough because vitamin D3 is also needed so your pet can process the calcium. Your turtle

Dandelion greens are high in calcium, which tortoises need to be healthy.

or tortoise gets vitamin D3 from full-spectrum light indoors or sunlight outdoors. You can add supplements, but proper lighting is a must.

Symptoms of metabolic bone disease include the softening or malformation of the shell and bones in the body. Because of a lack of dietary calcium, the chelonian's body is absorbing calcium from its bones and shell. This greatly weakens the animal, and it may drag itself along, rather than walk normally with its body lifted off the ground. The affected animal will die if something isn't done to treat it.

Be sure you're providing a balanced diet that includes vitamin and mineral supple-mentation (see chapter 6 for more info about diet). Always use full-spectrum lighting that emits UVB with any turtle or tortoise that is kept indoors. For more information about lighting, see chapter 4.

As explained in chapter 4, sunlight provides natural UVB, and it's great if you can give your pet turtle or tortoise time outside in the sun. Moving an indoor turtle cage next to a window won't do it because glass filters out the UVB rays (and at the same time, moving a glass aquarium

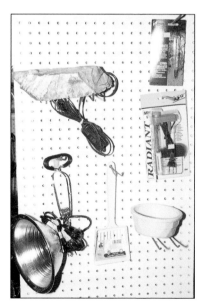

Using the proper equipment helps keep herps in tip-top condition.

Pyramiding

Pyramiding is a condition that causes a tortoise's carapace scutes to rise up to resemble a pyramid. An affected tortoise looks as if it's got a bunch of little pyramids on its back. Pyramiding is a somewhat mysterious condition, but it's currently thought that temperature and humidity play a role. It has been reported that too much protein and not enough calcium may also be a cause. Keeping your chelonians at the proper temperature and humidity levels and providing them with a healthy diet and the correct levels of supplementation (follow the instructions on the packaging) appear to be key to avoiding pyramiding. Any time you notice a shell deformity, though, it's smart to consult with a veterinarian.

next to a window in full sun could result in a cooked turtle). For the same reason, you don't want to place your full-spectrum lights over a glass cover on top of an indoor turtle tank (a glass top is a common feature over some aquariums). There should be nothing between the light and your turtles, except maybe for a screen top, if necessary to keep other pets or children from reaching into the tank.

If you notice your pet's shell is becoming weirdly shaped or soft, and if your pet seems sluggish and is not walking properly, it may be coming down with metabolic bone disease. And you know what that means: a trip to the vet.

Abscesses

An abscess looks like a swollen lump on your turtle's skin. It's common for an aquatic turtle to get an inner-ear abscess, which shows itself as a big bump on the side of its head. It can look pretty scary. An abscess can be caused by respiratory illness, poor **husbandry**, or both. (*Husbandry* refers to how you care for your pets. Good husbandry skills could mean you keep the cage clean, feed your animals properly,

Abscesses can look gross, but they are fairly common as well as treatable.

and so on. Bad husbandry skills may mean the water is left dirty, the temperature is incorrect, and the wrong foods are fed).

An abscess should be treated by a veterinarian, who will drain it and clean it. After treatment, there may be a wound on your turtle's head that you will need to keep clean. It may look gross, but it's better than leaving the abscess.

Shell Rot

More than other chelonians, aquatic turtles are especially prone to shell rot. When a turtle's shell becomes injured, perhaps by getting scratched or scraped against a rock, the injured area can become infected, possibly by dirty water. A bacterial or fungal infection can set in and cause further damage. Left untreated, your turtle's shell can become spotty, discolored, and soft in areas. It may even smell gross. Keeping your pet's water clean plays a strong role in the prevention of shell rot.

If your turtle becomes infected with shell rot, you will need to keep it out of the water and dry most of the time. Allow it to go into the water for a little while each day, though, so it doesn't become dehydrated. Treating the condition involves cleaning the affected areas, peeling away diseased sections, and administering antibiotics—all of which can be done by a veterinarian.

Turtles with shell rot need to be kept dry.

Salmonella

Pet reptiles, especially turtles, have been linked to cases of *Salmonella* (pronounced sal-meh-NEH-la) in humans, but the number of people who get sick from this because of their pet reptiles is small. *Salmonella* is the genus name for bacteria that cause a disease called salmonellosis, which can make you sick to your stomach, give you diarrhea, and cause other unpleasant side effects. It's most likely to affect small kids, senior citizens, and people who have a weak immune system.

The key to avoiding salmonellosis is to keep things clean. Whenever you handle your pets or anything that's inside their enclosures, wash your hands thoroughly with a disinfectant soap. The same goes for objects used with your turtles or tortoises such as food and water bowls, and cage decorations. Wash and rinse them thoroughly, and never handle any of your animals or their supplies in areas where they could come in contact with your family's food, such as near the kitchen sink. Don't put your turtles in any sink or bathtub, either.

Any time you're working with your turtles or tortoises or any of their supplies and equipment, clean up your work area completely. Don't give *Salmonella* even the teensiest chance to contaminate anything.

Because of *Salmonella*, the U.S. Food and Drug Administration made it illegal for people to sell baby turtles that are smaller than 4 inches (10 cm) in length. This is why you don't see baby turtles for sale in U.S. pet stores very often anymore. The law was put in place to combat possible *Salmonella* infection, which was linked to hatchling turtles that were sold as pets. What does 4 inches (10 cm) have to do with *Salmonella*? Turtles smaller than 4 inches (10 cm) were considered easy for young children to put in their mouths, thus leading to possible *Salmonella* infection! Personally, I'd never want to put a turtle in my mouth, no matter what the size. I strongly urge you never to do so, either.

Pictured are tapeworms from a turtle's stomach.

Internal Parasites

If your turtle or tortoise has diarrhea or its poop appears otherwise abnormal, consult with your veterinarian. Internal parasites, including different types of worms, can cause this. You might even see worms in the poop. Your vet may ask you to collect a stool sample so you can bring it in for analysis. (I know that sounds gross, but doing so will help get your pet well.) After determining what type of parasite, if any, may be troubling your pet, the vet will prescribe a medication.

Gout

You should know by now how important a proper diet is for pet turtles and tortoises. An improper diet can wreak havoc on your poor pet. Previously, you read about metabolic bone disease, which is caused by, among other things, an improper diet. Add gout to that list.

Gout is most commonly associated with plant-eating tortoises that are given too much protein in their diet. As a result, crystals form in the tortoise's joints, causing them to become swollen and stiff. This can be very painful, and injections of different medicines may be needed to relieve your pet's pain and remedy the situation.

Cracked or Broken Shell

Accidents sometimes happen, and your turtle or tortoise may end up with a broken shell, either from being dropped or from having something dropped on it. This is very serious, and you must get your pet to a reptile veterinarian right away. He may put a cast, made of fiberglass or some other hard material, on your pet's shell to hold it together until it heals.

Prevention

I hope you and your pets will never have to deal with the conditions mentioned in this chapter. If you take proper care of your turtles and tortoises, by keeping their habitats very clean (especially the water for aquatic turtles) and at the proper temperatures, and by feeding them the right foods and exposing them to the right kind of light, you hugely increase the chances that your turtles and tortoises will remain healthy. Even so, it's a good idea to have a knowledgeable reptile veterinarian lined up, just in case the need arises. If you're not sure where one is located near you, you can check the Web site of the Association of Reptilian and Amphibian Veterinarians at http://www.arav.com.

This snake-necked turtle has a cracked shell. A cracked or broken shell is very serious and needs to be treated by a veterinarian as soon as possible.

CHAPTER 10

Turtles in Trouble

A s you can imagine, living in nature (also known as the wild—with good reason) can sometimes be dangerous and a bit scary. You probably sleep in a comfy bed at night, inside a warm house with a roof over your head and loved ones snoring in other bedrooms nearby. You never have to worry about being plucked from your bed, tossed in a large box with a bunch of other people, and eventually sent to a market, where giants will buy you to use you as a primary ingredient in some soup.

Sea turtle

The populations of wild box turtles have been shrinking. This is why you should buy only captive-bred box turtles and not remove any from the wild.

Some wild turtles, however, do face that scary possibility.

There are many turtles and tortoises roaming about in habitats all over the world. Lots of them live their lives quietly, trundling around, eating, sleeping, hibernating, swimming, basking in the sun, and making baby turtles. Much of the time, they do this without interference from anyone.

Some wild chelonians, however, do encounter trouble, and unfortunately, these problems are often caused by humans. In this chapter, we're going to examine difficult situations that certain wild chelonians are facing. Some of this news is sad—but there is hope. We will also take a look at a number of the efforts that are underway to help turtles and tortoises survive.

The Asian Turtle Crisis

Some people who live in Asia enjoy eating turtle meat. And some of the Asian turtles being sold in Asian markets are endangered. Although Asia isn't the only place this happens, it's traditional for Asian people to eat these turtles, so it's not easy to get them to stop.

Turtles there aren't used just for food, either. They are also used as ingredients for medicine. China, because it's such a huge country with con-

Turtles are often sold in foreign markets—sometimes for pets, often for food.

siderable wealth, creates a big demand for "food and medicine" turtles. People in Southeast Asia catch the turtles and send them to China. Although the United States also ships turtles to China for the same reasons (as well as for pets), it does not ship any endangered species.

Some **conservation organizations** (groups of people who try to do what's best to preserve nature and everything in it)— including Conservation International, the Turtle Survival Alliance, and the Asian Turtle Consortium—work to help Asian turtles. They educate people in Asia about the problems their turtles face and raise Asian turtles in captivity so they can someday be released back into nature to help the wild populations increase. They also work with the appropriate agencies in Asia to try to set habitat aside where the Asian turtles can be protected. In addition, farms that raise turtles specifically for food purposes are popping up more often in Asia, making it likely that the need to take Asian turtles from nature will dwindle. This all requires much work and effort on the part of a lot of dedicated, turtle-loving people. If they could talk, I'm sure the wild turtles would thank them!

In the United States, especially in southern states such as Louisiana, people eat snapping turtles in soups and stews. You can even buy canned snapping turtle soup. Some turtles, including snapping turtles, are raised on farms especially for the purpose of being sold for food, just as cows and pigs are raised on farms before they end up on dinner tables as hamburgers, hot dogs, and other foods. Fortunately, snapping turtles are not threatened or endangered.

Another U.S. turtle, however, has been negatively affected by people's appetites: the diamondback terrapin (*Malaclemmys terrapin*, pictured above). This is a pretty turtle with white skin and black spots that is found in states along the East Coast of the United States. It has been hunted for its flesh, and today it's a threatened species. Conservation efforts in recent years, however, have helped the diamondback terrapin to increase its numbers in the wild.

Sea Turtles in Danger

There are seven species of sea turtle: the loggerhead (*Caretta caretta*), the hawksbill (*Eretmochelys imbricata*), the green turtle (*Chelonia mydas*), the leatherback (*Dermochelys coriacea*), the Kemp's ridley (*Lepidochelys kempii*), the olive ridley (*Lepidochelys olivacea*), and

All sea turtles are threatened or endangered species, and there are a number of reason why, from illness to parking lot lighting.

the flatback (*Natator depressa*). All of these turtles are either threatened or endangered.

There are several reasons the majestic sea turtles have become endangered. One has to do with the way sea turtles are born. Mother sea turtles come out of the ocean to lay their eggs in the sand on a beach. Lights near beaches can confuse female sea turtles, which can lead to eggs not being laid. Once eggs are laid, they may be eaten by predators, including people.

When the baby sea turtles hatch, hundreds of them scramble over the sand, trying to reach the ocean. Unfortunately, many never make it to the water. Baby sea turtles that hatch at night in wild areas where there are no houses or buildings are "programmed" to head away from dark areas because dark areas are inland, away from water. Instead, they instinctively head for the lightest area on the horizon, which is the ocean (especially if moonlight is shining on it). This behavior can become a problem when the turtles emerge from their nests on beaches that are near bright city lights, such as those that are found along streets and in parking lots. Because the baby

Although sea turtles live in the ocean, they do come on land occasionally, especially to lay eggs.

turtles think that the brightest area means that's where the ocean is, they head for the lights instead, and they can be killed by cars and other hazards. (Some towns are trying to make it a rule to turn off city lights that are near beaches where sea turtle nesting occurs, so the lights don't confuse the turtles.) And even if baby sea turtles are scrambling in the direction of the ocean, predators such as dogs, birds, crabs, and people may snatch them up.

Other dangers include people who have poached adult turtles (meaning they caught them illegally) for use in manufacturing products such as moisturizing lotion and combs

made from sea turtle shells. Fishing nets can snag sea turtles by mistake, too, entangling and drowning them. Although they live in the ocean, sea turtles do need to come to the surface to breathe air.

Sea turtles are also plagued by a disease called fibropapillomatosis (also known as FP), which causes tumors to break out both on and inside a sea turtle's body. The disease has been around for years, but it's been showing up more frequently, and people aren't sure why.

Luckily, people are coming to the rescue of sea turtles, too. Because of the problems trawling nets (used to catch shrimp) were causing, the U.S. shrimping industry got together with

There are a number of conservation efforts that seek to help sea turtles.

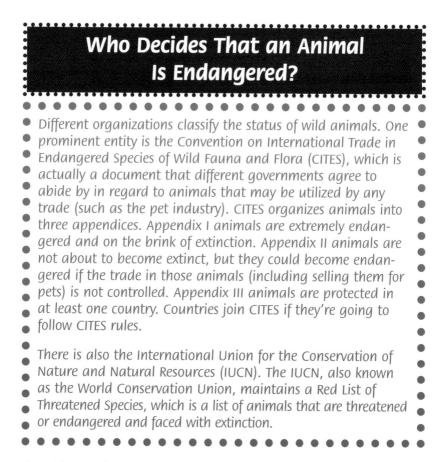

Who Decides That an Animal Is Endangered?

Different organizations classify the status of wild animals. One prominent entity is the Convention on International Trade in Endangered Species of Wild Fauna and Flora (CITES), which is actually a document that different governments agree to abide by in regard to animals that may be utilized by any trade (such as the pet industry). CITES organizes animals into three appendices. Appendix I animals are extremely endangered and on the brink of extinction. Appendix II animals are not about to become extinct, but they could become endangered if the trade in those animals (including selling them for pets) is not controlled. Appendix III animals are protected in at least one country. Countries join CITES if they're going to follow CITES rules.

There is also the International Union for the Conservation of Nature and Natural Resources (IUCN). The IUCN, also known as the World Conservation Union, maintains a Red List of Threatened Species, which is a list of animals that are threatened or endangered and faced with extinction.

the National Oceanic and Atmospheric Administration (a U.S. government organization that monitors oceans and the sky) to create a **turtle excluder device (TED)** that allows a turtle that's trapped in a trawling net to escape. TEDs are now being used in other countries as well.

There's even a hospital that specializes in treating sea turtles.

The Turtle Hospital, located in Marathon, Florida, helps many sea turtles. The staff there works to return them to the ocean after they've been treated for a variety of troubles they may have experienced, including sickness and injuries caused by encounters with boats and other dangers.

Nesting sea turtles are also offered protection as they lay their eggs, and boats may patrol the waters offshore to keep poachers away. There are conservation groups devoted to sea turtles, too, such as the Caribbean Conservation Corporation and Sea Turtle Survival League, which develop various programs to study and help the turtles. More research needs to be done to aid sea turtles, though. I hope they'll remain swimming in the ocean forever.

Disappearing Habitat

More and more people keep popping up on the planet, and they all need places to live. To find space to build homes for all of these folks, developers

Gopher tortoises are sometimes buried alive during building construction.

New housing developments often mean less habitat for wild herps.

clear natural areas of trees and pave the areas over. This sort of activity affects the habitats of turtles and tortoises as well as those of other animals.

Habitat destruction such as this is the biggest problem facing many animals today. As more and more neighborhoods are built, more and more natural areas in which turtles and tortoises live are wiped out. Some chelonians find places to live among the houses, such as in artificial lakes or ponds and in people's backyards. Many, however, are killed when the land is raked over and built up. In the

United States, box turtles especially are being affected, and the numbers of wild box turtles has gone down drastically over the years. And don't forget about the entombment of gopher tortoises that was mentioned in chapter 8.

The Plight of the Desert Tortoise

Wild desert tortoises are suffering from a respiratory disease called mycoplasmosis (pronounced my-koe-plaz-MOE-sis). Because this disease was found in captive tortoises before it was discovered in wild tortoises, scientists believe the wild animals were infected by pets released into nature. This is never a good thing to do. Never set a pet loose in the wild, whether it's a tortoise, a bird, or even a fish. The animal is likely to die, and it could also affect other wildlife in a bad way, as has apparently happened with the wild desert tortoise population in California. Tortoise owners are urged never to release their pets into the wild desert areas of that state.

Another threat to desert tortoises is people driving off-road cars and motorcycles. A popular place to zoom around in these vehicles is the desert, where desert tortoises live and can be run over and killed.

Desert tortoises, too, have their champions, however, and the U.S. Fish and Wildlife Service, the Desert Tortoise Preserve Committee, and other organizations (both public and private) do a lot to help and protect them. There are now places set aside for tortoises where it's illegal to take off-road vehicles and where fences are erected to keep tortoises confined to a safe area. There are also desert tortoise rescue and adoption centers, where you can adopt pet desert tortoises. Read about them in the "U.S. Tortoises" section in chapter 8.

It's Not Easy Being a Chelonian

It's definitely not easy being a wild turtle or tortoise in today's world. Let's all hope that the good people whose goal is to

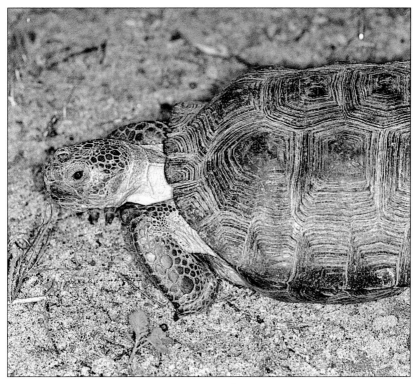

Not only should you never take a desert tortoise from the wild, but you should also never release a pet desert tortoise back into nature.

ensure the survival of the world's turtles and tortoises are successful in their quest. Most organizations accept donations, so perhaps you, as well as family members and friends, can help these groups help turtles. Check out the Web sites of the organizations that were mentioned in this chapter, as well as others that you may find by doing a little research (see page 126). You can even "adopt" a sea turtle at some Web sites when you make a donation—now that's a good way to spend some money!

I hope this chapter didn't bum you out too much. It's important to know the problems facing wild turtles and tortoises today and that there are good people who are working to help them. They *are* helping them, too, and there's increased hope for tomorrow's turtles and tortoises.

CHAPTER 11

Dos and Don'ts for Owners

T he following ten dos and ten don'ts will aid you when you want to get a turtle or tortoise and help you take care of it properly. All twenty are covered in more detail elsewhere in this book. I hope that you use them to make your experiences happy ones and that you and your chelonians are together for many years to come!

Egyptian tortoises

Play it safe by always washing your hands any time you handle your turtles or turtle-keeping equipment. Cleanliness is the solution to many problems.

Do read a lot and do a lot of research before buying a turtle or a tortoise.

Do buy healthy animals, including captive-bred specimens, whenever possible. Inspect the animals for signs of illness.

Do be sure to provide a large enough enclosure for your pets.

Do provide full-spectrum lighting for any turtles and tortoises that are kept indoors. Getting them outside in sunlight is good, too.

Do feed your turtles and tortoises healthy foods that are appropriate for them. Remember that turtles eat meat; tortoises don't.

Do give your pets proper levels of vitamin and mineral supplements.

Do keep your pets' enclosures clean (especially the water in an aquatic turtle tank). Doing so prevents illness.

Do be on the lookout for any signs of illness, and take your pets to a reptile veterinarian if you observe some.

Do take measures to keep chelonians that are maintained outside safe from cats, dogs, and other predators. Use escape-proof enclosures.

Do remember to always wash your hands after handling your turtles and tortoises and anything that may have been in their enclosures.

Don't buy any animal on impulse. This African spurred tortoise hatchling is super-cute, but it will grow into a huge adult that will need lots of space.

Don't buy any animal on impulse.

Don't buy a turtle or tortoise without knowing how big it will get.

Don't get any pet unless you are sure you can take care of it for as long as it will live—or maybe as long as you live!

Don't bring home a sick animal thinking you'll make it well.

Don't just stick a turtle in a tank and expect it to thrive without the proper care. Know what it needs before acquiring it.

Don't feed vegetarian tortoises protein.

Don't forget to provide a temperature gradient for your pets. Being able to choose a temperature helps them stay healthy.

Don't let your tortoises roam loose around your house. They can get into mischief.

Don't paint anything on any turtle or tortoise's shell!

Don't take wild box turtles or *Gopherus* tortoises out of their habitat.

And last but not least, here's one never:
Never *stop learning about turtles and tortoises!*

Glossary

aquatic: type of animal that spends most of it's time in the water

carapace: the top part of a turtle's or tortoise's shell

chelonians: another name for turtles and tortoises

Convention on International Trade in Endangered Species of Wild Fauna and Flora (CITES): a document that different governments agree to abide by in regard to animals that may be utilized by any trade

conservation organizations: groups of people who try to do what's best to preserve nature and everything in it

endangered species: species whose numbers are so few they are in danger of dying out

ectothermic: dependent on the environment to raise and lower body temperature

habitat: the area in which an animal naturally lives

herp: a nickname for a reptile; from the word *herpetology*, the study of reptiles and amphibians

husbandry: how you care for your pets

keel: a raised sawtooth-shaped structure that runs down the middle of some turtles' shells

morphs: animals with a special color or pattern

plastron: the underside of a turtle's or tortoise's shell

poachers: criminals who kill or steal wild animals

quarantine: to keep a new animal isolated from any other pets until you're sure it is free from illness

range: territory in which the different species of turtles and tortoises can be found

scutes: plates that form a protective layer on the shell

species: types of an animal

threatened: an animal that could become endangered if something isn't done to help its wild populations increase

turtle excluder device (TED): a device that allows sea turtles trapped in trawling nets to escape

Recommended Reading

Reptiles Magazine
A monthly publication covering herps from A to Z.
The Web site provides useful care tips as well as links to breeders,
photo galleries, and message boards.
http://www.reptilesmagazine.com
PO Box 6050 • Mission Viejo, CA 92690

Conant, Roger and Joseph Collins. *A Field Guide to Reptiles and Amphibians: Eastern and Central North America.* 4th ed. Houghton Mifflin, 1998.

Stebbins, Robert. *A Field Guide to Western Reptiles.* 3rd ed. Houghton Mifflin, 2003.

Web Sites

If you would like to support the people and organizations working to help endangered and threatened turtles, here are some places to start on the Internet.

Asian Turtle Consortium • http://www.asianturtle.org/

Caribbean Conservation Corporation and Sea Turtle Survival League
http://www.cccturtle.org/

Conservation International • http://www.conservation.org/xp/CIWEB/

Desert Tortoise Preserve Committee • http://www.tortoise-tracks.org/

The Turtle Hospital • http://www.turtlehospital.org/

Turtle Survival Alliance • http://www.turtlesurvival.org/

Other Internet Resources

California Turtle & Tortoise Club • http://www.tortoise.org/

Convention on International Trade in Endangered Species of Wild Fauna and Flora (CITES) • http://www.cites.org/eng/app/index.shtml

Melissa Kaplan's Herp Care Collection • http://www.anapsid.org/

Turtle and Tortoise Preservation Group • http://www.ttpg.org/

Turtles of the World • http://nlbif.eti.uva.nl/bis/turtles.php?

World Chelonian Trust • http://www.chelonia.org/

Photo Credits

COVER
Front cover (main image top and boxes): Paul Freed;
(main image bottom): Bill Love/Blue Chameleon Ventures.

FRONT MATTER
Title and Contents: Paul Freed.

CHAPTER 1
4: Zig Leszczynski. 5 (top): Mariea Holland. 5 (bottom), 6, 7, 8 (bottom): Paul Freed.
8 (top): Victor Habbick Visions. 9: Isabelle Francais.

CHAPTER 2
10: Allen Blake Sheldon. 11 (left and right), 13 (left and right), 14, 15 (top right, bottom
right, middle left, bottom left), 16, 17, 18 (top and bottom), 19 (three bottom images), 20,
21, 22 (top and bottom), 23: Paul Freed. 12: Photos.com. 15 (top left): Robert T. Zappalorti,
Nature's Photo Images. 19 (top): Zig Leszczynski.

CHAPTER 3
24: James E. Gerholdt. 25, 26 (top), 27, 28 (top and bottom), 29, 32, 33 (top and bottom), 35, 36,
37, 38, 40: Paul Freed. 26 (bottom): Allen Blake Sheldon. 27: Art Explosion. 30: Shutterstock.com.
31 (top and bottom): Photos.com. 34: Roger Klingenberg, DVM. 39: Photos.com.

CHAPTER 4
42, 43, 44, 45 (bottom) 46, 47 (top and bottom), 48, 49, 50 (top and bottom), 51, 52: Paul Freed.
45 (top): Philippe de Vosjoli. 53: Heather Powers.

CHAPTER 5
54: Photos.com. 55 (top, bottom left, bottom right), 56 (top and bottom), 57 (top and bottom),
58 (top and bottom), 59, 62, 64, 65 (top and bottom): Paul Freed. 60: Bill Love/Blue
Chameleon Ventures. 61: Heather Powers.

CHAPTER 6
66: Paul Freed. 67 (bottom), 69 (bottom), 70 (middle): Photos.com. 67 (top), 68 (top and
bottom), 69 (top), 70 (top and bottom): Paul Freed. 71: Russ Case.

CHAPTER 7
72, 83: Photos.com. 73, 74, 75 (top), 76, 77, 78, 79 (top and bottom), 80, 81 (top and bottom),
82, 84 (top and bottom), 85: Paul Freed. 75 (bottom): Allen Blake Sheldon.

CHAPTER 8
86, 87 (top and bottom), 88, 89 (top and bottom), 90 (left and right), 91, 92, 96, 97
(top and bottom), 99, 100, 101: Paul Freed. 93 (top and bottom), 94, 95: Photos.com.

CHAPTER 9
102, 106 (top), 109: Photos.com. 103, 104 (top and bottom), 106 (bottom), 108 (bottom),
110, 111: Paul Freed. 105, 108 (top): Roger Klingenberg, DVM.

CHAPTER 10
112, 113, 116, 117 (bottom), 119 (top and bottom): Photos.com. 114, 115, 121: Paul Freed.
117 (top): Niki Case.

CHAPTER 11
122, 123, 124: Paul Freed.

GLOSSARY
125 (left): Paul Freed. 125 (right): Zig Leszczynski.

ABOUT THE AUTHOR
128: Russ Case.

Stickers illustrated by Tom Kimball.

About the Author

Russ Case, pictured here with a red-footed tortoise, is the editor of the monthly magazines *Reptiles* and *Aquarium Fish International*. He also edits the annual magazines *Reptiles USA*, *Aquarium USA*, and *Marine Fish and Reef USA*. He lives in Southern California and has been a reptile and amphibian enthusiast since he was a small child exploring the wilds of suburban New Jersey in the 1960s.

Turtles & Tortoises Stickers

Can you find where to place these in the book?